Climbing Ice

Climbing Ice

Yvon Chouinard

SIERRA CLUB BOOKS · SAN FRANCISCO

IN ASSOCIATION WITH THE AMERICAN ALPINE CLUB

Photo page 1 by Tom Frost

Photo page 2 by Kathy Ryan

Library of Congress Cataloging in Publication Data

Chouinard, Yvon, 1938-
    Climbing ice.

    Includes index.
    1. Snow and ice climbing.   I.   Title.
GV200.3.C48   796.5'22   77-19137
ISBN 0-87156-207-3
ISBN 0-87156-208-1 pbk.

Address: 530 Bush Street, San Francisco, California 94108

To my mother and father, who gave me the freedom to pursue my chosen craft.

The south face of Huandoy, Norte Cordillera Blanca, Peru. Henry Kendall Photo.

A mountaineer may be satisfied to nurse his athletic infancy upon home rocks, and he may be happy to pass the later years of his experience among the more elusive impressions and more subtle romance of our old and quiet hills. But in the storm years of his strength he should test his powers, learn his craft and earn his triumphs in conflict with the abrupt youth and warlike habit of great glacial ranges.

Geoffrey Winthrop Young

Contents

This book was ready for publication in 1972 and again in 1973, and 1975 . . . but always publication was put off because there had to be revisions to keep abreast of the changes in the state of the art of ice climbing. That's one trouble with writing about an evolving art—you can never really feel finished. The ice revolution is still continuing, but I feel that most of the existing techniques will still be in use ten years from now, and I hope most of this text will still be valid. There will be great changes in the equipment, however, particularly in the hardware and tools. For this reason I've avoided placing too much emphasis on specific gear. As long as one has the technique down, switching from one tool to another won't cause any great problem.

Most people these days take up ice climbing after they are already accomplished rockclimbers. In keeping with this tendency this is not a book for beginning climbers. Much of the technique and the terminology of ice climbing is quite esoteric, and if you were to attempt to learn climbing solely from this book, there would be gaps in your experience, particularly in the basics of rope management and belays.

Until the 1970s the countries in the world where snow and ice climbing was practiced were divided into those that used only flat-footed (or French) cramponing techniques and those that climbed on the front points of the crampons. Both schools of climbing were equally proficient, but neither side was willing to admit the worth of the other's technique. It is possible to do all your ice climbing with only one technique—as many persons still do—but it is not the most efficient way nor does it make for a very interesting experience. It is like knowing only one dance. When the music changes, you are still dancing, but rather out of tune. So, as is usually the case in these matters, the truth lies right down the middle. Now all the best ice climbers know and apply both methods in their cramponing.

In this book I have included all the valid methods of climbing on snow and ice and have attempted to place them in proper perspective. For the sake of clarity each technique is described separately and in its pure form, even though in practice one doesn't always climb with a single pure technique. For instance, changing directions on steep ice with French technique is much easier to do if you switch to your front points to turn instead of straining your ankles to keep all the points into the slope. Yet by learning to do these techniques in their pure form you can progress further as an all-around ice climber than if you start taking the easier shortcuts too soon. With time and experience will come the synthesizing of all these separate techniques into one's own personal style of climbing. No book should attempt to do this for you.

When first I began work on this book eight years ago, I never dreamed that it would become such an albatross. Over the years, I've worked on the manuscript in spurts of frenzy interspersed with long periods of laziness, frustration, and guilt. Climbing has been easy for me; writing is difficult. I have to strain, and sweat, and grunt out each word. It don't come easy.

My friend Dan Doody once warned me about what it was like to write a book. He had just come back from an adventurous year in South America where he did a new route on Chacraraju in Peru and had explored some uncharted jungle rivers. He was writing to me from his room at his parents' farm in Connecticut. "I'm holed up here for the next four months working eight to ten hours a day on this damn book. It's hard to believe that just a few weeks ago I was sitting in my dugout canoe in the middle of the Amazon with this brown-skinned woman who was only wearing a skirt made from fiber that she spun and wove with her own hands. I've decided that this sitting around and writing is all bullshit. The only thing that counts is the self-discipline."

Well, Dan, those words have pulled me through my periods of funk time and again. Perhaps the reason I climb is to prepare myself mentally and physically for the hardships of writing!

Certainly the chore would have been much more difficult without the help of several friends. There was Doug Robinson, who helped a lot with the writing. I'm grateful to André Contamine for getting me enthused on French crampon technique through his writings in various journals.

I'm indebted to John Cunningham for turning me on to the many original techniques that he has worked out over thirty years of climbing and particularly for revealing to me the subtleties of front-pointing.

Mike Moore, formerly of *Mountain Gazette*, worked on the design from the stages of rough layout to the final design. There were many persons who lent me their valuable photographs, some of which I have held onto for years. I thank them for their trust and patience.

I apologize to Ed LaChappelle for using so much of his work on avalanches.

I can only cite ignorance of the facts and the need to be brief for leaving out of the history chapter persons and events that may be at least as deserving as those mentioned.

Yvon Chouinard
November, 1977

Tom Frost Photo.

The traditions of climbing have always been important to me, and I usually have great respect for the achievements of the climbers who preceded me. After repeating a classic climb I would often be left amazed at the difficulty and seriousness of a route done years before—a route done without benefit of modern hardware, guidebooks, or specialized training. And, of course, the pioneers had to carry that heaviest burden of all: the fear of the unknown. I looked for guidance in my climbing career to heroes like John Salathé, Emilio Comici, Jack Durrance, and André Contamine. Being of a new, "hot" generation, however, my peers and I could go into a new area, repeat the classics in record time, and, before leaving, put up one or two new routes which were harder than the classic. So we often didn't have too much respect for the existing standards, particularly of routes which had been done by climbers whose names were unknown to us.

Mount Alberta has a reputation for being the hardest peak in the Canadian Rockies. The first ascent was done way back in 1925 by a couple of Swiss who were guiding a group of Japanese gentlemen. In 1958 it had been climbed only three times and carried an aura of impregnability about it. Ken Weeks and I had been climbing for several months in Yosemite and the Tetons and were in super shape. Therefore, we had plans not only to knock off Alberta but to do it by a new route—a long, steep icefall leading up to an easy but graceful snow ridge.

The Sunwapta is one of the worst rivers to cross in the Rockies; it's ice cold, wide, and fast. Because it's fed by glaciers and snowfields, the only chance to cross it comes in the cold early morning. Weeks and I were really poor that summer; all we had to eat for three weeks were sixty pounds of potatoes and carrots and a bag of flour which we had scrounged from an old Canadian Alpine Club base camp. The extra-heavy packs actually kept us from floating away as we "ferry-glided" the river.

Further along, Habel Creek proved to be a rat's maze of bushwhacking and loose scree slopes; we had to cross and recross the creek many times. Late in the second day we arrived at the glacier at the base of the mountain. It was the first time we had ever been on a real live glacier, and since it was the only flat place around, we made our camp right on the ice. All night long we were kept awake by loud snaps and pops as cracks shot across under our sleeping bags. We were scared shit-less because we didn't know if the cracks might suddenly open all the way up into a big crevasse!

We were going to do our new route right, so we got off to an alpine start, a remarkable feat for two Teton rockclimbers. All day we cramponed up and down little ice cliffs, bashed steps up seracs, and jumped across crevasses *à la* Bob and Ira Spring photos. At last we were real alpinists! On the summit snow ridge we moved together, carrying coils just like Gaston Rébuffat does in his books. We literally ran the last few hundred feet to the summit. The tin-can register said: "Mount Woolley, 11,170 feet." Over to the west, barely visible through the approaching storm, we made out the enormous, evil-looking Alberta.

I
A Brief History of Ice Climbing

The Early Years

Ice climbing may be older than western civilization. Watercolors from that cradle of culture, China, show fourth-century B.C. men climbing on rock, so who can say that Han Shan (the T'ang Dynasty lunatic who left his poems carved on cliffs) was not out tiptoing on the ice in the moonlight? We'll never know.

We do know that the earliest journeys on ice from which we feel a heritage were made by those medieval Alpine shepherds who crossed passes with their three-point crampons, steel-tipped staffs, and perhaps a woodcutter's axe to form steps. The first outsiders who seemed to notice these crude techniques were the Englishmen who had been flocking to the high mountain resorts in the early 1800s. The English gentry were beginning to develop a peculiar passion for mountains, and the shepherds soon found it more profitable to herd gentlemen than sheep. The shepherds became guides, and their staff and axe merged into one tool, at once chopper and balancing stick. This early ice axe, along with their growing skill and confidence, took the shepherds and their tweedy charges up and down many a glacier and snow climb since canonized as "classic."

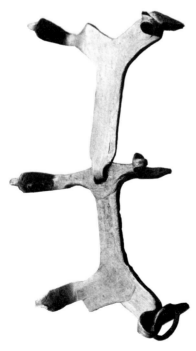

A pair of old, handmade crampons. Opposite, the Diamond Couloir on Mount Kenya. Tom Frost Photo.

A Brief History of Ice Climbing

By the mid-nineteenth century the "stairway to the stars" period was in full swing as guides cut hundreds of large steps on snow routes so that their clients would encounter no traumas. An exemplary climb of the time was the Brenva Spur on Mont Blanc, climbed in 1865 by the guides Jakob and Melchior Anderegg and their clients. This climb was not technically harder than others of the day, but it represented a psychological breakthrough, for the crux of the difficulties is a barrier of unstable ice blocks near the end of a long, remote route.

This step-chopping era that flourished during the last half of the century was also the golden age of guided climbing. No gentleman took to the hills without his guide (or guides, often three or four to a *Herr*!), and a porter was handy for bringing the white wine for the summit celebration. So the guides ended up doing the routefinding and cutting the stairways of steps, which required the brute strength the gentleman client usually did not possess. The practice led to such aberrations as Christian Klucker's cutting a line of steps up the Bodile Couloir in preparation for a client's ascent which, scheduled for the following day, never materialized.

Klucker couldn't have minded too much, for unlike most of the guides he was a passionate climber and was certainly the outstanding mountaineer of his time. His two greatest climbs, the Piz Rosez and Lyskamm north faces, are still considered serious undertakings.

As the century was ending, a new style of climbing was in the making, and Alfred Mummery was its harbinger. His career was brilliant in several ways, beginning with his rejection of guided climbing (such as the first guideless ascent of Mont Blanc's Brenva Ridge). Once, while attempting the Aiguille du Plan, he led an ice pitch so steep that he needed to cut handholds to stay in balance while he chopped steps. But Mummery was primarily a rock-climber, and that emphasis was also prophetic at the turn of the century, for the avant garde of the mountaineering world was already turning to rockclimbing. The British on their home crags had elevated climbing on rock from a practice to an end in itself, and in 1910, an expatriated American, Oliver Perry-Smith, was leading very difficult and unprotected sandstone in Germany. With its laborious stepcutting, the fickle and often dangerous snow and ice was left behind for the more glamorous and dynamic rock, which anyway was closer to the essence of climbing—the ape swinging from limb to limb.

Losing the limelight to rock acrobats didn't really bother the Europeans living at the foot of the Alps. The British gentlemen had started something, and now it would be carried on by French,

The renowned Engadine guide, Christian Klucker, photographed by J. Gaberell in 1922.

German, Swiss, and Austrian climbers. The summits had been reached, the long snow slogs had been put in, but there remained steeper and more frozen ridges and faces waiting to be climbed.

During these years, that heavy and unwieldy instrument which had chopped so many steps was refined considerably. The cutting blade of the ice axe, called the adze, became perpendicular to the handle, and the shaft was shortened for better swinging balance.

Renaissance

In 1908 a radical development changed snow and ice climbing forever: an Englishman named Oscar Eckenstein created a ten-point crampon. Like the ice axe, the concept of crampons did not spring full-blown from the Victorian mind; shepherds had their spiked horseshoes, and four-point crampons were well known at the end of the nineteenth century. The new crampons of Eckenstein met with considerable hostility from the Victorian mountaineers, for they felt that this new development took an unsporting advantage of the peaks. This attitude may seem a little incredible today, but our modern context interferes. We relate to the mountains through rubber-soled boots, the natural outgrowth of today's concentration on rockclimbing. Great for gripping the rock, they are also good in soft snow. But they grow more useless as the snow freezes and steepens. The Victorian climbers wore nailed boots which took slippery snow in stride, and they stood confidently in airy lines of steps for hours behind a chopping guide. What's the use, they must have thought, of even longer spikes? It was just as natural for them to take off their nailed boots for steep rock pitches and climb in stocking feet as it is for us today to fit on crampons for frozen snow. Eckenstein wrote, "Like most British climbers I have always scorned the use of these invaluable articles, a scorn which was entirely based on ignorance and prejudice. However, I have learnt better. . . ." The reluctant Victorians had failed to perceive that crampons weren't just sissy nails but instead held the potential of doing away with steps. The weary-armed guides, however, could see that quite well. Indeed, Eckenstein claimed that because of his crampons he never cut more than twenty steps in his career.

In the end Eckenstein's crampons carried the day. He was the first to work out the flatfooted cramponing technique which today is generally known as the "French method," though many climbers still call it the "Eckenstein technique." He claimed to be able to walk up 70-degree ice with no other aid, though he may have been

To counteract the slipperiness of the ice; they firmly attach to their feet shoes resembling the shoes of horses, with three sharp spikes in them, so that they may be able to stand firmly. In some places they use sticks tipped with iron, by leaning upon which they climb steep slopes. These are called alpine sticks, and are principally in use among the shepherds.

—Simler, 1574

A Brief History of Ice Climbing

pushing both the angle and the soft end of what can really be called ice. (Even today there is considerable difference internationally in what is meant by the term "ice.")

So, while the English cherished their rock climbs, cramponing up steep snow and ice was catching the fancy of French mountaineers. Cramponing flatfooted so fitted the huge faces of frozen snow of the French Alps that the French developed it into what today is still the most subtle and graceful form of the ice climber's art. Not only did they have Eckenstein's crampons, but to go with them they had another of his designs, the first functionally short, lightweight ice axe—it was 86 centimeters long, two-thirds the length of the usual axe.

Ice climbing was now on the verge of its most productive era. From the first days of the new crampons on into the 1930s, hundreds of long climbs were established on the huge snow faces of the Alps. These routes have become synonymous with the very name of alpine climbing.

Jacques Lagarde at the doorway of the old Argentière hut.

Hans Lauper was the last of the great guides to be raised in the old tradition, and he was the first to tackle the big north walls of the Western Alps. He managed to do eighteen major first ascents between 1915 and 1932, including the north faces of the Kamm, Mönch, and Jungfrau. He also climbed the beautiful and difficult route on the east flank of the Eiger which now bears his name. In the French Alps, Jacques Lagarde and Henry de Segogne were the first to push the Eckenstein crampon technique to its limits. In 1924 they did the extremely difficult north face of the Aiguille du Plan, which Mummery had attempted. This steep face of water-ice has been repeated only a few times since. With Camile Devouassoux, Armand Charlet, the Argentière guide, climbed the difficult Nant Blanc face of the Aiguille Verte in 1928. Charlet was to remain the leading French ice climber until the late 1940s, and he was the person most responsible for developing modern crampon technique.

In the thirties the focus shifted to the Eastern Alps and the emphasis to mixed climbing. The center of activity was Munich, a city where nearby boulders offered practice climbing before and after work. Consequently, the Munich men became excellent rockclimbers, and when their holiday came around they would bicycle through the Alps, picking off the plums. So the brothers Schmid got off their bicycles in Zermatt one summer day in 1931, walked up and climbed the north face of the Matterhorn, first of the three famous "last great problems" of the Alps to fall. Riccardo Cassin and his ropemates shortly accounted for the next problem: the Walker Spur on the Grandes Jorasses. This left the north wall of the Eiger, for years a Munich monopoly; it was finally climbed in 1936.

The North Wall Era produced many great climbers, but the real genius of the age was the Munich climber Willo Welzenbach. Like most of the Bavarian climbers, he started out as an excellent rockclimber. But like Lagarde and Charlet he preferred mixed rock and ice climbs, and his first big success came in 1924 on the northwest face of the Gross Wiesbachhorn, which proved to be the most difficult ice course yet done in the Eastern Alps.

For three years Welzenbach was unable to climb because his arms were weakened by tuberculosis. Several operations left his right arm partly paralyzed, but he nevertheless returned to the biggest walls of the Bernese Oberland in 1930 and climbed the north face of the Gross Fiescherhorn. In the next three years he made the first ascents of five more of the biggest walls in the Oberland. In 1931 he and Willy Merkl climbed the steep north face of the Grand

Above, Hans Lauper, the photo borrowed from Mountain *Magazine.*
Below, a rare photograph of Armand Charlet, demonstrating 'Charlet technique' on the Bosson Glacier, Mount Blanc.
J. Minster Photo.

A Brief History of Ice Climbing

Willo Welzenbach on Nanga Parbat.

Charmoz. A terrible storm broke when they were partway up. Refusing to descend, they waited out the worst of it and continued on in very bad conditions to reach the summit on the fourth day.

Nineteen thirty-two was Welzenbach's greatest year. On the north face of the Grosshorn, victory wasn't won until after two bivouacs and an uninterrupted line of steps for 1,200 meters. In the same year, Welzenbach, Alfred Drexel, and Erich Schulze climbed the northeast face of the Gspalterhorn without using a rope in order to move faster and more safely, for there was much rockfall danger and the shattered rock offered poor belay spots. A day or two later, in the middle of a rainy afternoon, they threw themselves on the virgin north face of the Gletscherhorn. They endured a fierce bivouac and reached the summit the next afternoon, during another storm. Four days later, with Schulze, Welzenbach ascended the north face of the Lauterbrunnen Breithorn. Thus, in eight days of poor weather, he managed the first ascents of three dangerous and extremely difficult north walls.

The greatness of this era lay not so much in the length and serious-ness of its climbs as in the style of execution. For example, André Roch and Robert Greloz climbed the north face of the Triolet with no protection whatever; Lauper's route on the Eiger was made in the same manner. Today we occasionally lead without protec-tion because placing it can be more precarious than continuing; our ultimate security now rests with a dependable nylon rope. The pioneers were using hemp, and its "ultimate security" is sum-marized in the admonition that "the leader must not fall."

Technical equipment was undergoing changes during this period. Fritz Riegele designed special pitons for use in ice; they were first used on Welzenbach's 1924 ascent of the Gross Wiesbachhorn. In 1932 Laurent Grivel added two front points to the then-standard ten-point crampon. These new twelve-point crampons were enthusiastically adopted by the German and Austrian climbers. Once, on a climb on the Aiguille Verte, two separate parties were climbing the steep Whymper Couloir. One group was laboriously chopping steps when, to their astonishment, the other team (of which Grivel was a member) quickly passed them using the new crampons. Shortly after Grivel's crampons made their appearance, Austrian ice climbers began to weld a bar across the hinge of the crampon, thus making a rigid design which better suited the harder ice of the Eastern Alps. But these technical advances did not detract from the climbers' commitment of hurling themselves onto Alpine walls in bad weather with unreliable hemp ropes, no down gear (only wool clothing and potato sacks for bivouacs!), and, of course, no helmets or use of fixed ropes. By the mid-1930s this golden age of north-wall ascents reached a height of boldness and commitment which may never be seen again.

In 1942, two young French climbers, Lionel Terray and Gaston Rébuffat, made an ascent of the Col du Caiman, a relatively short but very steep water-ice gully. In recounting this climb many years later, in his book *Conquistadors of the Useless*, Terray cast a reflection which catches much of the technical tenor of the pre-war era: "Now in those far-off days practically no one practiced the delicate art of walking up ice slopes in balance on their crampons. The rule was to start cutting steps as soon as the slope reached about thirty-five degrees, a harrowing and painfully slow proceeding. Personally, I did crampon up reasonably steep angles, but without using my axe in the anchor position which I later learnt from my master, Armand Charlet. My poor axe position did not allow me to realize the full possibilities of my crampons, and on hard ice forty-five degrees was almost my maximum. . . ."

Out of the Mainstream: The Scots

During the 1940s the Alps seemed climbed out of ice, and attention shifted both there and worldwide to the large-scale artificial rock routes which would dominate the climbing world for the next twenty years. During this time of general eclipse and relative calm, however, ice climbing was flourishing in the Highlands of Scotland. Actually it wasn't pure ice climbing but rather a uniquely Scottish sport that was eloquently described by Professor Norman Collie in his 1894 *Scottish Mountaineering Journal* account of the first real Scottish winter climb, the Tower Ridge: "And what joy, think ye, did they feel after the exceeding long and troublous ascent?—after scrambling, slipping, pulling, pushing, lifting, gasping, looking, hoping, despairing, climbing, holding on, falling off, trying, puffing, loosing, gathering, talking, stepping, grumbling, anathematising, scraping, hacking, bumping, jogging, overturning, hunting, straddling,—for know ye that by these methods alone are the most divine mysteries of the Quest revealed?"

The Scots had always formed the most vigorous and outrageous backwater of the climbing fraternity, and with their delight at being contrary to fashion, it amused them to keep alive the art of tiptoing on ice through the age of rockclimbing and pitoncraft. Of course, the Scots had already been at ice climbing for some time; winter climbing was a major objective of the Scottish Mountaineering Club when it was formed in 1889. Its moving

Robert Greloz on the first ascent of the north face of the Triolet in September, 1931. André Roch Photo.

A Brief History of Ice Climbing

force, W. W. Naismith, declared, "If in the Alps the tide of fashion sets toward rock climbing, to the neglect of snowcraft, those of us with conservative instincts will, by encouraging ascents in snow, have the gratification of helping in some way to stem the prevailing current." Hard on Naismith's heels came the remarkable Harold Raeburn. Doubtless inspired by the now established and uniquely Scottish attitude that snow, ice, and blizzard—known as "full conditions"—were essential ingredients for a good day on the hill, he took up the cause of winter climbing with unbounded enthusiasm. Ranging extensively across the Highlands, he made his mark on every major outcrop in Scotland. His classic ascents include Crowberry Gully in 1893, in full conditions of course; Green Gully on Ben Nevis in 1906 in a blizzard; and Observatory Ridge in 1920.

Since the great snow and ice faces of the Alps were not to be found in the relatively gentle Scottish Highlands, the locals had long known that the gullies which cut the major massifs presented a fearsome, icy sight in winter. The great surge of creative gully climbing that was soon to sweep through Scotland extended the art of front-pointing which began when Grivel added two extra points to the front of each crampon. From this time on, harder and steeper ice could be climbed without tediously cutting steps; this manner more approached the freedom of rockclimbing. The Austrian and German climbers were quick to adopt twelve-point crampons, but the French, who were doing so well flat-footed, held out until much later. The Scots carried front-pointing and step-cutting into their sinuous and confining chimney-gullies and eventually onto iced rock climbs. The standards set by Raeburn remained until December of 1950 when, as the great ice climber Jimmy Marshall put it, "From dark Lochnager's icy crucible emerged a vital force: Tom Patey. His initiation, the fearful terminal wall of the Douglas-Gibson Gully, put him on the right road and set an example for all 'granite heads' to follow." Through most of the fifties Patey was the outstanding climber on the eastern crags of the Cairngorms and Lochnager. Marshall has written more on the history of this era: "To the west, in Glencoe and Ben Nevis, little was done in the early fifties, possibly because there was an already established legacy of splendid climbs to test the mettle and polish, the technique of climbers. A notable exception to this pattern was Hamish MacInnes (he's always ploughed his own furrow) with his ascents of Raven's Gully (1953), Rannock Wall, and Clachaig Gully." The first of the big gully climbs on Ben Nevis was done in 1957 "when Patey and Greame Nicol fell in with MacInnes to climb Zero Gully. The mountain and the men were

Harold Raeburn leading a rope on the Central Couloir, Ben Lui. A. E. Robertson Photo.

Opposite, Tom Patey in the lead on the Alladin Buttress, Cairngorms. John Cleare Photo.

Following pages, "Ben Nevis, the most massive, malevolent, most elevated lump of rock on these islands, is itself an island, humping hideous flanks from endless bogs, hard to equal for hidden depths and character." The description is by J. R. Marshall. The photo by Hamish MacInnes.

A Brief History of Ice Climbing

in good nick, and a splendid ascent was made in five hours, as fast as is ever likely for three men. . . . Old Patey, now ensconced in the fastness of the North West Highlands, embarked upon a momentous accumulation of solo and accompanied ascents around that region, with occasional forays South to pluck better quality routes from the cliffs of Creag Meaghaidh."

The real genius of the decade, however, was Jimmy Marshall. Starting in 1959, with the ascents of Parallel Gully B on Lochnagar and Smith's Gully on Creag Meaghaidh, he went on to completely dominate Scottish winter climbing. He was the "grand old man," the master under whom many of the best Scottish alpinists (such as Robin Smith and Dougal Haston) had their apprenticeships. Even today there probably isn't a climber in the world who is capable of bettering Marshall's style on Scottish ice, given the same tools—a long ice axe and a pair of crampons.

Above, the "Fox of Glencoe," Hamish MacInnes, tunneling through the Cornice on Ben Nevis.
Below, Jimmy Marshall on Parallel B Gully. Graham Tiso Photo.

The high-water mark of Scottish ice climbing crested in 1960 with Marshall and Smith's epic week on Ben Nevis. The pair made six major new ascents, along with the second ascent of the infamous Point Five Gully. Two of the climbs, Gardyloo Buttress and Orion Face Direct, were destined to be as difficult and as classic as any of the recent Scottish ice climbs. All that remained after 1960 was a mopping up of hundreds of lesser gullies, smears, and icy faces throughout the Highlands.

Allan Fyffe, one of the best of the modern Scottish climbers, describes the flavor of the old style winter climbing technique:

> Ice was attacked with an ice axe (usually blunt), and a ladder of steps of various shapes and sizes was hewn up the offending obstruction. This system sufficed for about eighty years, permitting winter ascents to be made of almost all the major gullies, chimneys and ice falls, together with many of the major buttresses. But it had its drawbacks: it was time-consuming and it demanded a fair degree of tenacity. A Grade 5 climb, for example, would take between five and eight hours, a long time to spend in a gully in the face of avalanches, falling ice chips, spindrift and retreating circulation. Crampons, when they finally took over from nailed boots, made a difference; steps no longer had to be cut everywhere, and most snow slopes could be quickly dealt with. In fact, front pointing of a sort was practiced: easy angled ice was often climbed using the two forward pointing and the first two vertical points, which gives a fairly stable platform. But this technique was generally confined to short pitches, easy angles, or sections of ice near the top of a pitch when it was used as a last resort before falling off due to lack of strength! Coupled with the then limited ways of belaying on snow or ice, plus the generally poor protection, it failed to make winter climbs any more attractive to those of a normal frame of mind.

Post-war Alpinism

The Alps in the 1950s and early 1960s saw little advancement in the technique of climbing ice, although a few climbs were made that were more difficult than any done during the North Wall Era. The outstanding climbs were the dangerous Bonatti/Zapelli route on the Eckpfeiler, the Cornauau/Devaille six-day ascent, in 1955, of the north face of Les Droites, and the 1968 Demaison/Flematti route on the Grandes Jorasses' "Shroud." The Droites

Nick Noon on one of the early attempts of Point Five Gully, Ben Nevis, in 1952. John Cunningham Photo.

A Brief History of Ice Climbing

Erich Friedli, Jr. Ruedi Homberger Photo.

route was probably the most difficult ice climb in the Alps until perhaps 1971, when the Cecchinel/Nomine route was done on the Eckpfeiler. The most significant change during this period, however, was in the time taken for the routes. In the late fifties and early sixties a young Swiss machinist named Eric Friedli repeated all of Welzenbach's Oberland climbs and accomplished a series of solo ascents of many of the classic ice faces of the Eastern Alps. All of these routes were done in remarkably fast time. He used pure front-pointing technique with hand-held ice daggers, but the difference was not technique but rather boldness. In 1969 Reinhold Messner, a native of South Tyrol, combined boldness and an athlete's training regimen to achieve an amazing nine-hour solo ascent of the north face of Les Droites. He was back in Chamonix for lunch, or so the story goes.

The sixties were the age of super nationalism in alpine sports. This was especially true in skiing, where there were Austrian, French, and even American techniques. The French, with their ten-point crampons, were artfully angling and flat-footing their way up the big snow faces of the Mont Blanc Range, while the Austrians and Germans were tiptoing around on only their front points. In 1969 the leading spokesman for ice climbing in France, André Contamine, wrote in the journal *La Montagne*, "The *piolet ancre* is one of the most useful techniques of the alpinist. It permits him to cover ground on the steepest slopes without fatigue or difficulty. It is the key to cramponing 'French style.' " Two years later the Austrian climber Wastl Mariner wrote in the same journal, "The most natural technique anatomically and the most secure and sparing of energy is to advance on steep ice on the front points of twelve point crampons—called front pointing." He went on to criticize the French technique for being unnatural and difficult to learn. This caused an absolute furor at the *Ecole National de Ski et Alpinisme* in Chamonix when rebellious students posted the article on the bulletin board!

However, by 1971 ninety percent of the better French climbers confessed to using the front-pointing method in climbing steep ice. Their Gallic pride was soothed, however, by watching the rest of the world quickly adopting the French ski technique! Today, primarily through Contamine's teachings at the French guides' school and through his writings in various journals, the French crampon technique is taught in climbing schools all over the world. After Lagarde and Charlet, Contamine was the master French ice climber. His ice axe design, the *Super-Conta* by Charlet, was the first to have a hole in the head; it was also the first to have deep teeth on the pick for a more secure anchor.

Developments in North America

Snow and ice craft came late to North America. At the turn of the century, Conrad Kain moved from Austria to guide in the little-explored Canadian Rockies. Mountaineering in this wild region was of necessity styled after the tradition of the old American mountain men. Kain needed a string of horses, a bear rifle, and plenty of navigational sense just to approach the peaks. His career culminated in the first ascent in 1913 of Mount Robson, jewel of the Rockies. Still a long and serious climb today (the sign of a good mountaineer is if he has climbed it by any route), it was not repeated for decades. Nothing as significant was done on ice for a long time, as Americans with their late start fell right in line with the worldwide interest in rockclimbing. There were a few good climbs done in the fifties and sixties in Alaska and the Canadian Rockies; the first was Mount Deborah in 1954 by Fred Beckey and Heinrich Harrer; this route involved a long and dangerous corniced ridge. Even though there were many attempts, the second ascent was not accomplished until 1975. Two other significant routes were the Emperor Ridge of Mount Robson in 1961 by Tom Spencer and Ron Perla, and the north face of Robson in 1963 by Pat Callis and Dan Davis. Except for a few Alaskan climbs, the difficulty and seriousness of these routes was no greater than what had already been done in the Alps in the twenties and thirties. In the eastern states a few ladders of steps up Mount Washington's Huntington Ravine marked an active day.

In 1964, the North America Wall on Yosemite's El Capitan was climbed; this event culminated the big-wall rockclimbing phase with the assurance that given enough time and equipment any rock wall could be climbed. Soon a micro group of Yosemite expatriates began shifting their attention to North American ice. In the same typically technocratic fashion that they had approached big walls and artificial climbing, Americans began to examine the tools of ice climbing.

On a rainy summer day in 1966, I went onto a glacier in the Alps with the purpose of testing every different type of ice axe available at the time. My plan was to see which one worked best for *piolet ancre*, which one was better at step-cutting, and why. After I found a few answers, it took the intervention of Donald Snell to convince the very reluctant and conservative Charlet factory to make a 55-centimeter axe with a curved pick for the crazy American. In those days a 55-centimeter axe was crazy enough—but a curved pick! I had the feeling that modifying the standard straight pick into a curve compatible with the arc of the axe's swing would allow the pick to stay put better in the ice. I had noticed that a standard pick would often pop out when I placed my weight on it. My idea worked, and a few years later Rob Collister wrote in *Mountain*, "The development of a curved pick for axes and hammers was an event in ice climbing history comparable to the introduction of crampons in the 1890s, or the use of front points and ice pitons in the thirties. It could prove more revolutionary than either. Since it makes for both greater speed *and* greater security, it will encourage those who have previously been deterred by the need to choose between the two."

The curved pick and deep teeth on the axes and my later-designed hammers definitely did provide a more secure anchor in the ice. A climber could support his entire weight on the axe and it wouldn't come popping out. This meant that, armed with one of these tools in each hand, the ice climber could attack vertical or even overhanging ice without chopping steps or using artificial aid. This strenuous technique was first done in the winter of 1967 in California and was later named *piolet traction* by the French.

In 1967 Tom Frost and I not only designed a new "alpine hammer" with a drooping pick, but also brought out an adjustable, rigid crampon made from chrome-molybdenum steel. Armed with these new tools (and with the reliable Salawa tube screws), American climbers began approaching steep ice with a new attitude. The couloirs of California's Sierra Nevada proved to have fantastic climbing in the autumn months when the summer snows matured into runnels of live water-ice. Over the years Doug Robinson and I took advantage of the lack of interest by others in climbing ice and scooped up the first ascents of many fine Sierra gullies. In Montana, Utah, Colorado, and the eastern states, summer waterfalls were discovered frozen in space from December to March. The game soon evolved into doing climbs in their "worst" conditions: that is, solid blue ice.

Coming of Age

By the end of the 1960s only a few groups were doing high-level ice routes. In Scotland a new super-climber had supplanted the legendary Jimmy Marshall. His name was John Cunningham, and he was pushing the limits of the front points at angles of up to seventy degrees. At this degree of steepness the hands could take advantage of natural holds, just as in rockclimbing. In 1970, he and Bill March from Glenmore Lodge climbed the short but plumb vertical Chancer on Hell's Lum in the Cairngorms; it was the first vertical Scottish ice climb to be done without chopping a ladder of steps.

At a time when older climbers were unwilling to adapt to the new ice gear and the younger generation was too impatient and narrow-minded to appreciate any technique *but* front-pointing, Cunningham showed an amazing versatility in developing, adapting, and modifying snow and ice techniques from all over the world to suit Scottish conditions and his own unique style of climbing. After the Marshall era he was certainly the dynamic force in Scottish winter climbing.

In 1970 curved picks and rigid crampons were introduced to Scotland by Doug Tompkins and me; using the new tools, we knocked off the desperate Direct Finish to Raven's Gully in Glencoe.

Previously, the difficult Scottish gullies were the domain of only an elite few, but the new equipment soon made these climbs so democratic that even the average ice climber was queuing up at the base of Point Five Gully. Allan Fyffe describes a special day: "Ian Nicholson and Dave Knowles set off up Zero one morning but neglected to rope up. An hour later, Nicholson emerged at the top, shortly to be followed by Knowles. The pair then descended to Point Five, and Knowles picked up another climber to do that route in fast conventional style. Nicholson, on the other hand, climbed the route in fifty minutes and then descended to the Fort for a lunch-time drinking session! This was probably one of the best mornings of winter climbing ever seen on the Ben, or anywhere else in Scotland for that matter."

The early 1970s saw the curved pick, front-pointing, and Hamish MacInnes' "Terrordactyl" (a specially shaped ice hammer) universally accepted for climbing steep ice. New routes which were considerably more difficult than any of the old classics were being established everywhere in the world. The word had even gotten to New Zealand, where in 1971 Bill Denz and Brian Pooley climbed the severe and remote Balfour Face of Mount Tasman. On Mount Kenya in 1975, Mike Covington and I straightened out the Diamond Couloir route by going straight over a vertical cliff in its midsection. In the Alps climbers discovered that the horrible dark couloirs which were death traps in the summer offered superb winter climbing. In 1972, after spending no less than thirty-one days on the Grandes Jorasses and using fixed ropes from a British attempt, a team of Japanese climbers succeeded in climbing the Central Couloir. It wasn't done with elegant style, but because of its length (1,200 meters) and the fact that it was done in winter,

A Brief History of Ice Climbing

this route must rank as difficult as any ice climb in the world. The northeast couloir on the Dru was also done in winter in 1974 in four days by Walter Cecchinel and Claude Jager. (Amazingly enough, this gully has since proved to be a reasonably safe summer route.) Another magnificent steep ice runnel, known as the Super Couloir, on Mont Blanc du Tacul, was climbed in May of 1975 by Jean Marc Boivin and Patrick Gabarrou.

The summer of 1975 saw most of the extremely difficult ice climbs in the Alps such as the Dru Couloir, the Shroud, and the north face of Les Droites, done without bivouacs by the better climbers. All the classics were regularly being soloed in very fast time. One young climber even waited until after the afternoon thunderstorm to start up the Swiss Route on the north face of Les Courtes; he went on to make the summit by six o'clock!

Most of the recent advances in ice climbing in the Alps have been confined to the French Alps, largely because of the British influence, which is not felt as strongly in Switzerland or the Eastern Alps. By the mid-1970s ice climbers in the French Alps were seeking out narrow, hidden gullies which snaked down between the great rock faces. A typical climb of this genre (and probably the most difficult) was the 1976 ascent by Alex MacIntyre and Nick Colton of the gully which lies between the Central Couloir and the Walker Spur on the Grandes Jorasses. At times this gully necks down to less than a meter wide; the climbing is very Scottish-like, but on an alpine scale. MacIntyre has described the climb in *Mountain*: "The only line that remained was the one that had been attempted by Bonington and Haston [they had reached a point 250 meters from the top on a 1972 winter attempt]. It had been described as a line too cold for ethics. But it was a good line, one to be followed rather than constructed, taking the easier way rather than avoiding it; a classical sort of line, but in the modern idiom. And, above all, it was a line without end, a plumb line."

During these frenetic years of activity, climbers were not ignoring the great ranges of the earth. European traffic in the Himalaya had been increasing steadily, but the kind of heavy trail-breaking typical of these expeditionary climbs was no more a contribution to ice climbing than was their sadly increasing experience of the relentless instability of Himalayan icefalls. The Andes, too, were slowly getting climbed, but also by heavy plodding in soft snow toward dangerously corniced summit ridges. It was not in these ranges that the ice-climbing standards of the seventies were being set.

The north face of the Grandes Jorasses. Chris Bonington Photo.

Opposite, on a winter ascent of the north face of Les Droites. Alex MacIntyre Photo.

31

The coming of age of eastern American ice climbing began in 1970 with the first non-step-cutting ascent of Pinnacle Gully on Mount Washington by Jim McCarthy and Bill Putnam. Good ice has been found in all the New England states and New York, not to mention eastern Canada, which is a vast untapped freezer. The outstanding climbs of the seventies have been John Bouchard's solo first ascent of the Black Dike on New Hampshire's Cannon Mountain, and John Bragg and Rick Wilcox's climb of the fierce Repentance on Cathedral Ledge.

In the western United States the climbing of frozen waterfalls took on an air of seriousness to rival even Scottish winter climbing. No longer were these smears, bulges, and frozen cascades merely practice areas for climbers honing their technique for the summer ice faces and autumn couloirs—it had become an end in itself.

The first really important waterfall to be climbed was probably Mahlen's Peak Waterfall, done in 1971 by Greg Lowe and a partner who belayed and jumared. The crux of this Utah classic was twenty meters of absolutely vertical ice capped by a five-meter overhanging section. This was probably the first time anyone had done such a long vertical section on hard water-ice without chopping steps or using artificial aid.

In 1974 Jeff Lowe and Mike Weis accomplished one of the most difficult waterfall climbs of the era—the delicately beautiful Bridalveil Fall near Telluride, Colorado. Much of the climbing was vertical and Lowe describes the crux in an article aptly titled "The Cold-Dance Review": "Mike led the crux, which was a three-foot roof with giant icicles drooping from the lip. For 20 feet he climbed the slightly overhanging wall below the roof and then knocked a hole in the curtain of icicles. Next he delicately bridged between the base of the icicles on either side of the hole, got the pick of his axe in above the overhang and muscled his way up. Following, it seemed equivalent to 5.10 rock climbing. We were both laughing and amazed at our success when we reached the top; we now knew we would never have to consider any ice climb in terms of aid."

In California, two Yosemite rockclimbers, Kevin Worral and Mark Chapman, on only their third ice climb, made an all-free ascent of the 300-meter high Widow's Tears, the first of Yosemite's waterfalls to dry up in the summer.

In western Canada a group of emigrated Britishers, led by the Scot Bugs McKeith, used siege tactics, bolts for belays, and artificial aid during the first ascents of a number of steep and extremely

Repentance and Remission, Cathedral Ledge, New Hampshire.

Opposite, the Grand Central Couloir on Mount Kitchener, Canadian Rockies. The crux is most often the verglas-covered slabs where the couloir necks down.

A Brief History of Ice Climbing

difficult waterfalls. The longest and most serious was probably Polar Circus on Peak 10,460; it was done in seven days by Allan and Adrian Burgess, McKeith, and Charlie Porter. The climb is nearly one thousand meters long and involves climbing several vertical sections.

Winter temperatures tend to stay extremely low in the Rockies in the winter, making for brittle ice and great powder-snow avalanches, but these disadvantages are more than made up for by the fact that many of the waterfalls are only minutes away from the highway. The trend in Canada now is to free climb the waterfalls in better style.

The finest ice climb yet done in North America is the thousand-meter Grand Central Couloir on Mount Kitchener in the Canadian Rockies. It was done in the summer of 1975 by Jeff Lowe and Mike Weis, who took twenty-six continuous hours to overcome the difficulties of overhanging bergschrunds, verglas, rotten snow on top of rotten ice, and steep water-ice.

Opposite, Bridalveil Fall in Colorado.
Bart Chandler Photo.
Below, one of Willo Welzenbach's finest climbs, the north face of the Grand Charmoz.
Bradford Washburn Photo.

A Brief History of Ice Climbing

When I was seventeen, I completely rebuilt a 1940 Ford two-door sedan and drove it from California to the Wind River Mountains of Wyoming. Across the Mojave Desert my old Ford and I purred past brand new Buicks and Cadillacs that were pulled off to the side with their hoods up and motors steaming.

When I drove up to Pinedale, Don Prentice was waiting for me. He was the one who had initiated me into climbing by teaching me rappelling for the purpose of obtaining falcons and hawks for falconry. My only climbing experience thus far was innumerable rappels, hand over hand climbing down a rope to falcons' eyries, and a lot of scrambling on the sandstone rocks near Los Angeles.

From our camp at the head of the Green River we all went out early in the morning to find a way up Gannet Peak, the highest point in Wyoming. The others climbed up a rock gully, but I struck off by myself up the west face. For most of the day I wound my way up chimneys, gullies, and short but steep rock cliffs. This was my first mountain, and I had no idea that they were so big!

The last cliff gave way to a long snowslope leading to the "gooseneck" and the summit. I was relieved to get off the face, as it had occurred to me that I could never get down the same way. The snow was hard with a soft slippery surface the way it gets on an afternoon in early June. I had no ice axe and my Sears-Roebuck work boots were smooth-soled and couldn't get a purchase on the snow. To the west a thunderstorm was brewing, and suddenly I felt very small and very alone; I decided to go down.

The descent began with an exposed traverse across a snowslope just above a three-hundred-meter cliff; then the way led down an even steeper snow gully to the talus below. I began to carefully kick steps across, trying to stay in balance. But as I became scared, my body would unconsciously lean in too far and my worthless boots would slip out of their steps. Several times I was stopped just short of falling by digging my fingers like claws into the slope.

That day I learned quite a lot about the insidious effects of fear and about plunging my heels down with vigor and depending on balance and on my legs for security. Most of all, this outing taught me that a confident attitude can often substitute for equipment and experience.

Climbing that first mountain over twenty years ago instilled a passion in me for climbing on snow and ice that continues to this day. I have noticed that most climbers are a product of their first few climbs. A person who learns his climbing on small but difficult crags may take up big-wall climbing or become an alpinist, but his first love will always be free climbing on the crags. I have specialized at one time or another in practically every form of climbing, but always I have been happiest to return to the snowy mountains to stand with one foot on ice and one on rock.

2
Climbing Snow

Characteristics of Snow

One of the joys of climbing comes from a growing intimacy with the medium. Learning rockclimbing has been described as a process of becoming increasingly sensitive to the forms of the rock. Technique follows awareness, and climbing on snow and ice takes more awareness because it is so much more complex and variable than rock. Not only must we be concerned with the outward form and texture of snow but, as we will be putting boot, axe, and crampons *into* it, we are also affected by how it has aged and packed, how firm is the crust, and how solid is the underlying snow supporting it.

Snow is infinite in its variety. Eskimos of the Canadian North have a dozen words that describe newly fallen snow in relation to how it affects the running of their sleds. The climber too comes to think of it functionally, classifying it according to the technique he uses to climb. These are not absolute categories but relate only to our climbing interests. If I were waxing for ski touring or downhill racing, predicting avalanches, or studying glacier formation, I would probably classify snow and ice differently.

The *firnification* process by which newly fallen snow (containing as much as ninety-seven percent air!) is transformed to hardpacked snow and ultimately to ice is extremely complex because it is

Opposite, climbers on the east ridge of the Doldenhorn. Bradford Washburn Photo.

affected by variable forces like wind, sun, and temperature. In fact, gravity is the only predictable force the new snow will encounter.

Newly fallen snow can be either wet or dry. The wet form obviously contains a large amount of water; the dry form is the skier's opiate, powder. Soon after falling, the delicate crystals of the new snow are tossed and mashed both by wind and the effects of gravity. Consolidation takes place rapidly, but the bonding of the new crystals, as well as the bonding between the new snow and previously fallen snow, can be affected by many factors, one of which is wind. The wind will compress the new snow on windward slopes, thus forming *wind pack*. The wind will also scour ridges and deposit some snow on the lee side; this then becomes an unstable mass called *wind slab*. On high ridges and exposed slopes, wave-like forms on dry snow are also caused by the relentless scouring of wind; these formations are known as *sastrugi*.

On steep terrain the newly fallen snow will often avalanche before it has had time to consolidate. Loose snow periodically pours down gullies and steep slopes, packing and scouring the slopes below (good step-kicking snow can often be found in an avalanche pack).

The ice climber is naturally concerned about the surface characteristics of consolidated snow, for that is where his feet must find their purchase. The sun's heat, in conjunction with the night's frost, will form a *sun crust* on new snow which, when it won't support the climber's weight, is called *breakable crust*. The wind can form *wind crust*, which can harden through compaction and age.

The melting of the snow pack by solar radiation, warm temperatures, and effects of the wind and rain, will gradually metamorphose new snow until coarse, rounded crystals form on the surface. When this surface is repeatedly exposed to melting and refreezing, it becomes *corn snow*.

Soft snow is all snow that gives under body weight. At the opposite end of the scale is *hard snow*, which can hardly be scratched even by a hefty kick. *Firn snow*, or *névé*, is summer snow which has survived at least a year. It is totally consolidated and can be hard in the morning and slushy by mid-afternoon. It offers ideal full-penetration cramponing when it is hard and equally fine glissading when the sun has done its work.

Suncups are hollows in the surface of the névé which are caused by both the sun's radiation and the evaporation from dry winds. At high altitudes suncups will leave pointed columns slanting toward the midday sun like worshippers praying toward Mecca. These columns are called *névés pénitants*.

Pick

Adze

Shaft

Ferrule

Spike

The leash on this axe has been hitched around the shaft to provide a secure grip on steep ice.

The Ice Axe: Primary Tool

I have already described the evolution of the ice axe from a long walking aid into a functional tool with subtle and sophisticated facets. The axe is the tool which makes progress on snow and ice possible. Throughout this book, as form follows function, each requirement of its shape will emerge from a new demand of technique.

At first, on gentle snowslopes, you need only an aid to balance—a cane, a third leg—so beginning requirements are only that the ice axe be the right length and sharp at its end. This bottom point, called the spike, must be sharp for positive grip on the ice, which means it should not be used as a cane on the approach trail and through the talus. For snow climbing, the spike should join smoothly into the shaft so it doesn't catch on crusty layers. The best shafts are made of laminated wood or fiberglass tubes. Metal shafts are strong but offer a cold grip and can be poorly balanced. Fiberglass shafts are light and strong, but, like metal axes, suffer from vibration problems. A laminated wood shaft dampens vibration best but is only half as strong as metal or fiberglass. Having an extremely strong shaft, however, is less important if you use the proper belay techniques which I will describe later in the book.

The length of an ice axe has been subject to the interpretation of every age. From the one-and-one-half meter alpenstocks of the pioneers, axes have shrunk to the 40-centimeter midgets seen in the early sixties in Scotland. Today the recommended length for general snow and ice climbing is 70 centimeters. This length is determined not so much by what makes a comfortable walking stick but rather how well the shaft balances the weight of the head and how well the axe can be plunged into a steep snowslope for a belay or support. The length of the axe is more dependent on the angle of the slope being climbed than a person's height. It turns out that the axe which is too short for a walking stick on the flats works out well on a moderate slope; the axe becomes useful at the angle at which it becomes necessary. Longer axes are indeed useful in places like Alaska, where unfathomable loose snow must be belayed in and probed for crevasses. Cutting steps downhill is also a traditional argument for longer axes. Conversely, a shorter axe

Climbing Snow

The axe held in piolet canne *position.*

of 50 or 60 centimeters is necessary for climbing very steep ice and for use in confined places like the Scottish gullies.

From the very start of your ice-climbing career you should cultivate the habit of holding on to your ice axe. It's important; you could be in serious trouble if you drop it! Victorians loved to tell stories of the leader, fatigued from hacking steps, dropping his axe. The second man watches it clatter down the face; then, making the significant gesture, hands the last remaining axe to the leader, who carries on to safety and the summit. There is a strong temptation to add a wrist loop to the axe to make certain it stays with you, but there are several disadvantages. Zigzagging up the slope, you will need to change hands on the axe at every corner to keep it uphill, and it is awkward and time-consuming to change the wrist loop as well. When you get on ice, the axe and hands will change positions so often while adapting to the changing terrain that a short wrist loop would be very impractical. Finally, in a severe, out-of-control fall it might be best to get rid of the axe rather than have it tied to your body. Remember, the axe is a cutting tool!

There are situations where a leash as long as the axe is not only useful but necessary: on a dangerously crevassed glacier where you could lose your axe in a fall; on mixed climbing where it's nice to let the axe hang from the leash while making a rock move or two; and in the winter on extremely steep ice where your hands are in clumsy mittens and the shaft is slick with ice.

One of the first questions a beginning ice climber asks is: How do I hold the ice axe? The answer is the first rule of ice climbing: Always hold the axe with the pick pointed forward, away from the body. This method is the opposite from what has generally been taught in the United States and Britain, but there are several excellent reasons for the practice. One is obvious: keep the pick away from the body so that in a slip or a fall it doesn't interfere with your digestion! The palm is placed over the adze, the thumb is held over the hole, and the forefinger is laid along the length of the pick. When correctly held, the pick is straight in line with the extended arm.

Upward Progression

Imagine how difficult it would be to learn to ski if none of the various turns were named. Well, thankfully, ice climbing has at last become sophisticated enough so that there are names and terms for the various positions of the feet and for holding the axe. Most of these names have become international; others I have thought

The steps illustrate the three foot positions in sequence: pied marche *on the flat,* pied en canard *on gentle slopes and* pied à plat *as it steepens. Tom Frost Photo.*

Climbing Snow

The two photos show piolet canne *with feet in balance and out of balance.*

up myself when necessary. It will probably bother some people that many of these names are in French. I won't apologize for this. The French are the ones who did most of the original work on the *pied à plat* (or French method), the names are theirs, and for the most part they would become exceedingly ugly and awkward when translated.

The French name for ice axe is *piolet (pyòlè)*, and all the positions for holding the ice axe will be introduced with this word. For instance, the previously mentioned technique of holding the axe like a cane is *piolet canne (kàn)*. Positions for the feet will be introduced with the word for foot, which is *pied (pyé)*.

When walking along flat or gentle slopes with the axe held like a cane and the feet in a normal walking attitude, the whole technique would be called *piolet canne, pied marche (màrsh)*. *Marche* is the attitude your feet are in when you are just walking.

When the slope gets steeper, it becomes more comfortable for the feet to splay out like a duck's. *Canard (kànàr)* is French for duck, so "duck-footed" technique would be *pied en canard*. Steeper yet, you will climb *diagonally*, keeping your feet flat by kicking horizontal steps. This *pied à plat (plà)*, or *"flat-footed"* technique, is the basis for all French technique. It is used on snowslopes because it is less tiring than kicking steps straight up.

The next unbreakable rule is that the ice axe is always held in the uphill hand. You will be using the axe for support and as a belay, so you might as well have an upper belay. For instance, suppose you are diagonaling up a steep slope, axe held in *piolet canne* by the uphill hand, feet in *pied à plat*. The shaft of the axe is rammed in with each couple of steps. It will be your security, so drive it in well and hang on to it. Should your feet slip, you must be stopped by the implanted axe. Don't lean into the slope, since this rips out the steps.

If, when climbing diagonally, the inside foot is forward, the body weight is equally distributed between both feet; this is called the *position of balance*. Outside foot forward is *out of balance* because all the weight will be on the lower leg. Since the ice axe is to be used as a belay, it is only logical to move it to a higher position when the stance is most stable: the *position of balance*. A rhythm soon develops: move the axe up, drive it in, step up out of balance using the axe as support, take another step back into balance, move the axe up, etc. As long as the axe can be securely rammed in above you and is only taken out when you are in balance, there isn't any need to belay with a rope even on the steepest snowslopes, for you are *self-belayed*. Most climbers don't ram the axe in with enough vigor to do them much good, and often the reason can be attributed to holding the axe with the pick backward. It becomes quite painful having the palm over the narrow pick. When correctly held with the pick forward, the adze creates a nice platform and prevents you from getting that creased, "monkey grip" hand.

When a diagonal ascent becomes tiring, you can switch directions (*zigzagging* or *switchbacking*). From the balance position, place the axe high and slightly to the rear and hang on to it for support. The outside foot takes another step, and the body turns to face the slope as the inside foot makes a step in the new direction. You are now facing the slope with feet splayed apart. Using the axe as a pivot, continue turning the body toward the new direction and bring the other foot through to the balance position.

On steep slopes a great disadvantage is noticed with an ice axe that is too long. It becomes very tiresome lifting a long axe so high and trying to ram the shaft in deep enough to do any good. On harder snow, of course, the problem is compounded; the axe is sticking way out, offering no belay at all. Too short an axe is not secure either, because it will rip out when the snow is soft and will cause the climber to lean into the slope on gentle angles. The importance of using the ice axe for self-belaying cannot be over-emphasized, and, if it is to be effective, you need a proper length axe, good balance, and a straight arm-and-shoulder follow-through motion accompanied with a vigorous attitude.

A direct ascent of a slope is faster but more tiring than the zigzag. When the snow is soft, you can face the slope and kick steps holding the axe in *piolet canne*, keeping it above you driven in the slope.

Piolet panne *and step-kicking on a slope just steep enough for two hands to be used for aid in balancing.*

Piolet manche. *Note the use of a leash from the axe to the waist tie.* (See Chapter VI.)

Climbing Snow

On moderate and steep slopes where the snow is hard, *piolet canne* gives way to *piolet panne (pàn)*. Facing the slope and holding the axe in normal *piolet canne*, stick the pick firmly in the snow about shoulder level. For steep slopes of softer snow, the head of the axe is held by both hands with the flat part of the shaft facing the climber. This technique, known as *piolet manche (mansh)*, allows a greater area of the shaft to grip the snow. When the snow is too hard to drive the shaft all the way in, one hand grasps the axe's head while the other grips the shaft near the snow surface. Again, I must stress the fact that the ice axe is the belay and is moved higher only when the feet are secure and the body is in balance.

Kicking steps is the normal footwork for climbing snow. The technique is obvious—just respond to the condition of the snow. In soft snow or snow with a breakable crust, the feet plunge in automatically; hard crust and frozen névé often take several kicks.

Piolet panne *and front-pointing on crusty snow on top of ice, photographed in the Karakoram at about 6,000 meters.*

At the extreme many vigorous kicks will barely make a nick to edge on with the toe or the inside of the sole. When soft snow has a hard base, a sliding-forward motion of the boot will create a more secure step.

As balance improves and confidence is gained in the ice axe self-belay, you will naturally start kicking smaller steps to conserve time and energy. Even granular ice can sometimes be climbed without crampons by taking advantage of bumps and rough patches on the surface. The next time you're on a "dry" glacier, consider leaving your crampons in the pack. If it's a fairly flat glacier and the ice is good and rough, you'll probably find yourself moving faster and with less effort than you would using crampons, particularly if it's early in the morning and the ice crystals are still sharp from sublimation.

When kicking steps in snow that is soft or rotten on the surface but still frozen underneath, crampons can help; their front points penetrate to the solid footing. They are a particular help, in fact quite necessary, when there is new snow on top of ice. But here step-kicking grades off into hidden front-pointing.

Means of Self-Protection

I have stressed the self-belay as a snow climber's first line of defense; use it well and you should almost never have to resort to a well-known technique called *self-arrest*. However, this "almost never" may mean just one time, and it may be an extremely necessary instance. For example, a mountaineer climbing or descending unaware into a patch of ice is likely to get himself upset suddenly and need a good means of stopping before he accelerates out of control. The self-arrest is not particularly instinctive but is rather a learned skill. A normal self-arrest is fairly simple to learn, but it quickly gets complicated in headfirst or tumbling falls. A slope can be so steep or so slick that unless you react quickly and in-stinctively and stop in just a few feet, you will have no hope of stopping at all. Thus, practicing the self-arrest over and over from every conceivable position is a must for the aspiring alpinist. An ideal practice slope is concave—steep at the top with a runout onto flat snow without rocks at the end.

"Shouldn't I always hold my axe with the adze forward so that I can go into self-arrest more quickly?" I hear this question often, mostly from those who have learned the "standard" but wrong way of holding the axe. It is certainly true that the climber doing a self-arrest must have his hand reversed on the axe's head, but this changeover shouldn't take more than half a second.

After making the reversal of the hand, the position in a self-arrest position is this: one hand grips the head of the axe with the thumb hooked under the adze; the other hand grasps the shaft down by the spike. The shaft is held diagonally across the body with the adze against the shoulder and the spike next to the opposite hip. The main principle of the self-arrest is to force the pick of the axe into the slope; this arrests your downward movement. The pick is pressed into the snow with the axe's head no higher than the top of the shoulder (if it is higher it will be much harder to hang onto). *Arch the body* so that its whole weight is on the toes and the axe. This is *the key to a good arrest* and is often neglected. You can remind yourself to do this by pulling the hand on the spike end of the axe away from the snow, forcing the body to arch and bear down on the pick. If you forget, the spike will probably remind you by catching in the snow and wrenching the axe out of your hands. Spread your feet for balance. You are stable on three points of support: an axe and two feet. (If you are wearing crampons, however, having your feet down will flip you over backwards, so you must use your knees instead. This will take some practice to remember.)

On hard snow be careful not to jam the pick in too quickly but rather do it dynamically, gradually putting on the brakes. The best way to do this, assuming you are not already sliding on your stomach, is to roll over toward the pick and come onto it gradually. If you roll toward the spike and catch it in the snow, you will lose your axe dramatically and suddenly. Try this on a practice slope and you will see!

Another major key to success with the self-arrest is this: Get into position as fast as possible. Do your first arrests on your stomach, then try quickly rolling into position from your back, remembering to roll toward the pick. Switch hands on the head and try again; you can't choose which hand your axe will be in when you fall. When you feel confident, go on to the interesting cases, headfirst-downhill and upside-down-and-backwards. The object will be to get rapidly from any attitude into normal arrest position, then stop. Sliding downhill headfirst, you will have the axe crosswise in front of you with the pick off to one side, trailing the shaft. Twisting the shaft to put pressure on the pick is like applying the brakes on one tread of a tractor—a rotation occurs. Your feet will start to slide around, pivoting on the braking pick until you are right side up in normal arrest position.

The psychological difficulty of throwing yourself over backwards downhill will be the hardest part of the next exercise. Once you are sailing downhill headfirst on your back and have gotten oriented, hold the axe across your waist with the pick off to the side and start applying the pick-brake. It helps if you can sit up at this stage. The brake will send your feet arcing off to the opposite side, and by pulling with your shoulders you will end up in normal arrest position. It will take some practice. The ultimate test-case is a tumbling fall, and in Bob Dylan's words, "I just said, good luck."

Descending Snow

On one early trip I learned to glissade from Fred Beckey. He was a hell of a skier and glissaded like he skied, standing up and angulating. The axe was either left in the pack or held in the air out of the way. Every evening in camp after supper Ken Weeks and I would go off during the "children's hour" to climb up and glissade down snowslopes for hours on end, always trying to link those turns together like Beckey.

One time in the Tetons, Fred and I were descending a granular ice slope on Mount Owen. A party which had started many hours ahead of us was slowly rappelling the slope, leaving ice piton anchors. Fred gave me his North Wall hammer, grabbed an angle piton for each hand, and dove headlong down the ice. Caught up in his enthusiasm, I followed as best I could. Those dudes almost fainted right there when they saw us go by. Later that night we were sitting around a soda fountain when the same blokes came in and started telling everyone about the madmen who glissaded an ice slope on Owen. That made our day!

Whenever possible, gentle, moderate, and even some steep slopes should be descended by the *glissade*. Not only is it a very functional

49

maneuver, but it can be one of the more enjoyable acts of mountaineering. Ideal snow for glissading is solid enough for support but softened on the surface. If the surface is rough and frozen there will be too much friction, and you will not be able to slide effectively even on steep slopes. Because of the need for a softened surface, late afternoon often offers good glissading; if you wait until the evening freeze sets, you may have to walk or even put on crampons.

To be good at the art of glissading, it helps to be a skier, but practice is more important. There are three basic methods: the *standing*, the *crouching*, and the *sitting glissade*.

Standing glissade. Tom Frost Photo.

Of these three techniques, the *standing glissade* is the safest, most enjoyable, and hardest to learn. A good mountaineer will use this method almost all the time. The technique is identical to skiing. The feet are together with slightly bent knees acting as shock absorbers; the weight is centered over the balls of the feet. Rock too far forward onto the toes and you can trip; weight centered on the heels will slow you down. The steeper the slope the more you must lean forward so as to get your weight over your feet. You can slow down by rocking back on your heels and even stop by turning your feet sideways and skidding; the best control, however, is by turning. Turns are initiated by rotating the upper body, and consequently the legs and feet, toward the new direction. Rolling your knees and ankles toward the turn will angle your boots onto their edges, thus helping carve the turn. Unweighting can help, too, especially on high-friction snow or low-angle slopes. It is accomplished by a crouch-and-spring-up motion and by turning on the downhill side of small bumps on the terrain.

I implied earlier that Fred Beckey did not use his ice axe while glissading. Many climbers of the "early American school" learned to be prepared for a fall while glissading; they were taught to hold the axe across the body in a pre-self-arrest position. Imagine how poorly you would ski if your arms were locked together holding an ice axe in self-arrest position. It would encourage you to fall, wouldn't it? To ski and glissade properly, the arms must be away from the body and free to swing and maintain rhythm and balance; thus the axe is held *piolet canne* like a ski pole.

If you don't lean far enough forward in a standing glissade, your feet will shoot out from under you, and you'll go out of control. Another problem arises when there is a sharp transition from one type of snow to another; you'll find this out when you run into hard clumps or little ridges of ice on an otherwise soft slope. In time, technique and confidence will correct the leaning-back problem, and experience alone will help you avoid those hard, usually darker patches of snow or ice.

When you get down to a low-angle slope, you might find that friction is stronger than gravity. To avoid coming to a full stop, you can take long, flat, *skating* strides much like a ski-tourer does. This technique is very good for picking up speed.

Imagine glissading along doing turns, holding on to the ice axe like a ski pole, the shaft pointed forward (not just dragging behind on the snow), and you hit a hard bump and start going out of control. Using your falling momentum to "straight-arm" the shaft of the axe in *below* your feet, you end up laid out on the slope

A standing glissade with the axe held *piolet canne, just as you would hold a ski pole.*

Climbing Snow

hanging on the head, stopped dead just a few feet below where you "blew it." The axe is usually held in the strongest hand and is rammed in using a stiff wrist-, arm-, and shoulder-driven motion. Think of a matador plunging the sword between the bull's shoulders.

"If I'm making a turn to the left, and I've got my axe in my right hand, won't I just trip over it if I try to ram it in?" I hear this question a lot. In correct skiing or glissading technique, the skis or feet may be going to the left, but the upper body is always facing the fall line; thus, keeping the axe in the strongest hand is valid.

This self-belay with the axe in glissading is not a technique you can pick up overnight. It will take a great deal of practice before it becomes instinctive and effective. You may not always be able to stop yourself at first, but at least by freeing your arms you will be in better balance and control. A good way to practice the self-belay stop is by doing a series of "foot brakes" and stops down a slope. The foot brake is accomplished by starting a turn, and then shoving the heels down hard into the snow and straightening the legs. Keep your feet together in the edging position. If they are apart, the top leg will be supporting all the weight, and, of course, two sets of edges or two brakes are better than one. With each stop, coordinate ramming in the axe down near your feet with your stiff arm, shoulder, and body weight. With proper timing your feet will brake and your ice axe will be planted all at the same time.

Slopes that are very dangerous from being either very fast, very steep, or having no runouts, can be safely glissaded by diagonal traverses; stop every ten or twenty feet with a foot brake for absolute control.

So much for the standing glissade. As I have said, it can be used *most* of the time. However, when a slope doesn't have a safe runout or is so steep as to preclude standing, the *crouching glissade* can be used (incidentally, I use this method to test a slope before I'll let loose with a standing glissade). The technique is essentially glissading sitting on your heels to keep the center of gravity low and close to the snow. It gives good balance and means you don't have as far to fall or as awkward a position to recover from if you do blow it. However, it is not necessarily a safer technique. In a crouch you have much less control over turning, and the foot brake is less effective. Your entire position is less dynamic and versatile, but at least you can use the spike of the axe as a brake and, should you fall, you are closer to a self-arrest.

Preparing to do a foot brake and glissading self-belay, the axe should be thrust in at a point below the feet so that by the time you stop, the axe and feet will be together in one reinforced anchor.

Opposite, crouching glissades. Tom Frost Photo.

Climbing Snow

Coming down the "Otter Slide," a 1,000-meter-long gully in the Karakoram.

In the crouching glissade the axe is held like the brakeman held the brake stick of an old-time toboggan. This is *piolet ramasse (ràmàs)* or "ice-axe brake." The flat of the shaft faces the fall line because the less taper in the spike in this position will help brake better. Keep the pick away from your face, and make sure that the hand that is on the shaft is close to the surface of the snow to eliminate leverage. On very steep slopes, take a diagonal line and brake with the axe and the feet.

When the snow is too soft to slide on with your feet, you can sit and go down in a *sitting glissade*. Wearing wind pants will improve your acceleration; you can also tuck your cagoule between your legs and use it as a seat. If you still can't get moving, the last resort is to lay all the way out flat on the snow. This will get you down many a soggy slope; know your runout since this is the hardest position to see from. A slope that is prone to wet snow avalanche can often be best descended by picking a trough that has already avalanched once or twice, starting another slide and keeping on top of it the whole way in a sitting glissade.

As soon as you are a bit nervous about glissading a particular slope, don't do it! It's slower but safer to go down soft snow facing outward and dig the heels in with a stiff leg (*plunge-step*). Use the weight of your falling body to dig in those heels; only an aggressive approach is truly safe. On moderate slopes the axe shaft is partially stuck in with each step in such a way that if the feet should slip, the axe can quickly be rammed in deeper. On steeper slopes the axe is rammed in all the way as far below you as possible; then two distinct plunge-steps are taken before the axe is moved lower. Again, the climber is self-belayed when he is most likely to fall.

Whenever you feel uncomfortable going down facing out, switch around and face in, kicking steps while holding the axe in the *piolet manche* position. A great deal of time and effort can be saved with no sacrifice of security by taking the longest possible steps.

An expert alpinist would think nothing of plunging headlong down the famous snowfield on Canada's Snowpatch Spire, his ice axe held out like a ski pole and his perfectly linked turns taking him right up to the brink of the three-hundred-meter drop. For the average climber to take a chance like this, however, is foolhardly. Never throw yourself onto a slope before testing the quality of the snow. Where there isn't a safe runout, use extreme caution. Questionable passages can be glissaded roped, the climbers leapfrogging down one at a time. The *hip axe belay*, discussed in Chapter 6, can make this maneuver go very fast.

Plunge-stepping down at a slight diagonal makes it easier to place the axe well down, allowing you to take a maximum number of steps below before removing it.

"In France we say that the third time is always lucky." So we were greeted by the guardian of the Argentière refuge in the Mont Blanc massif. Layton Kor and I had been there twice before in futile attempts to do the north face of the Aiguille Verte, and always the weather had turned us back. Nineteen sixty-six had been a disastrous summer for weather. None of the big, classic mixed routes had been done except the Walker Spur of the Grandes Jorasses, climbed with eight bivouacs by a slightly more than enthusiastic Japanese team. Though it was already the beginning of September, and Kor and I had been climbing all summer, neither of us had yet bagged one of the big ice climbs for which the Alps are so famous. Pressed for time now, we were willing to stick our necks out a little if given reasonable conditions.

I hardly had time to lay down my rucksack before Layton stepped out of the hut with an armload of beer. Sitting on the terrace, we watched the alpenglow leave the tops of some of the greatest ice climbs on earth: the Triolet, incredibly steep and dangerous-looking with its hanging seracs; Les Courtes, 900 meters of ice and ice-covered rock; Les Droites, the most difficult ice climb in the Alps, whose first ascent took five days and whose third ascent was done only in 1966. The first 250 meters of this route are 55- to 60-degree ice over unclimbable rock slabs; belays are often impossible because of the thinness of the ice. Last to lose its golden crown of glow is the second highest peak in the French Alps: the Aiguille Verte and its Couturier Couloir, the least difficult of the great north walls of the Argentière basin.

The Verte was our goal—but the sky was too blue and conditions too good; with the sun hardly down, it was already below freezing. No, we could always do the

Verte. We should go for something really big—maybe the Courtes. The guardian's son mentioned that the North Face Direct had been done only six times, a testimonial to its difficulty when one considers that a fearsome climb like the Triolet has probably been done a hundred times.

Midnight. I toss and turn in bed, my eyes wide open. I can't sleep and get more and more angry because I *have* to sleep! There is only another hour before we have to leave the hut. Kor is having the same trouble, and so in a fit of anger we grab our gear and bolt out into the moonlight. The glacier crossing is no problem with such a bright moon. At the bergschrund we eat an early breakfast, or is it a late supper? We rope up ten meters apart and move together. Kor goes first with his headlamp, ice axe, ice dagger, and crampons: the tools of the ice climber. My world is a small square of 50-degree frozen névé; beyond is darkness. Above, another light moves at the same speed. Stick in the dagger, plant the pick of the axe, kick in one crampon, then the next—the German technique, efficient but extremely tiring on the legs and not nearly as sophisticated or varied as the French. A hundred and fifty meters of 50-degree hard snow goes quickly when you move together.

It is three o'clock and bitterly cold, and we gloat over our new double boots. Since the snow has turned to ice and steepens considerably, we start to belay. We scale two pitches of 55- to 60-degree white ice partly by chopping steps and partly by front-pointing. We do two more fantastic 60-degree leads all on our front points with piton belays. The dawn reveals wild exposure. The 50-degree slope above looks like a ramp compared to what we are on. Although the angle has eased, we continue to belay and place ice pitons because the exposure is so awesome and our legs are so tired. Occasional pieces of ice come zooming by, so I fix a line from my waist belt to the ice piton that I am using for a dagger. Should I see a rock or hunk of ice coming, I can quickly drive in the piton.

We have to cope with three kinds of conditions now: hard snow, water-ice, and powder snow—these change every ten meters. With aching calves both of us by now are disenchanted with the front-point technique and vow to learn the French method before we try another climb like this. Switching leads is no longer practical, because by the time we arrive at the leader's stance our legs are too tired to lead on. One man leads for three pitches, and then we switch. Lack of sleep, severe dehydration, and the altitude have us moving like snails. On the summit I am completely exhausted. On the descent Layton belays me down all the ticklish spots. There is obvious avalanche danger (two people were killed on these same slopes a few days ago), but we have no choice except to go down. We pick an avalanche trough, start a slide, jump on top, and ride it out, going right over the filled-in schrund, too tired to be afraid or to enjoy it. At nightfall we reach the Couvercle refuge; it has been a hard day's night.

Climbing Snow

3
Climbing Ice: The French Method

Flat-footing

When the snow becomes so hard you cannot kick steps, you must either cut them or put on crampons. Cutting steps is more efficient for short distances, cramponing faster in the long run. The French call their cramponing technique *pied à plat*—literally, flat-footing —because it is just that; the feet are placed flat on the slope all the time. The natural terrain for this technique is the hard frozen snow (névé) or soft ice of the Western Alps, where crampon points will penetrate easily, or at least without too much kicking. *Pied à plat* also works nicely on water-ice at modest angles.

Unlike front-pointing, the French method is difficult to learn. It is a subtle, sidelong approach to the ice, yet when mastered it is a most efficient way to climb. There are few alpinists in the world who are true masters of the pure French method. The difficulty lies in developing a sense of balance and adhesion. One relies on three points of support, yet to advance it is necessary to remove the third point of support. This leaves the body delicately balanced, and only an exactly correct technique will leave one feeling secure. It takes practice to develop this sense of balance-adhesion, and the technique must be constantly refined as the ice steepens. The average climber must, and rightfully should, resign himself to applying the French method only on moderate slopes. So why bother with it at all when front-pointing is so simple and easy to learn? The French technique does have certain advantages over front-pointing. It is less tiring on the calf muscles because the feet are kept flat. It is more secure on soft or rotten ice because the climber's weight is spread out over more crampon points; there is less chance of them shearing out. On descents French technique most closely approximates the natural facing out or sideways attitudes familiar on rocks. Its disadvantages are its limitations on very steep or very hard ice and, of course, its difficulty to learn.

Ice-climbing technique varies according to the quality of the snow or ice, the steepness of the slope, and to some extent, the fitness of the climbers. By being able to choose from more than one technique, the climber can switch around whenever one set of muscles gets tired. That great Yosemite rockclimber Chuck Pratt once told me that he thought that there is more freedom in ice climbing than in climbing rock because you're not so limited in the range of techniques that can be used for a certain problem. A 50-degree slab of frozen névé can be climbed using any number of different tools and techniques. I've been on pitches where I've had to change techniques a dozen times to keep up with the varying conditions. But whether you are on rock or ice, isn't moving over constantly changing difficulties with proper technique, grace, and composure what climbing is all about?

Characteristics of Ice

Ice can be formed directly from water freezing, or indirectly through the continuing metamorphosis of névé, whereby the snowpack becomes more dense. The medium is called ice when its mass becomes airtight.

All ice in which crampon points will easily penetrate can be called *soft ice*. The ice which is in the next stage of hardness from névé is *snow ice*, which usually forms the transition layer between névé and serac ice. Snow ice is often found on the surface of a slope of harder ice.

Rotten ice or *granular ice* is made up of poorly bonded spherical crystals and is usually found on sunny slopes or on lower glaciers in the summer, when the temperatures are high during the day and barely freezing at night. When the spherical crystals are well bonded, the ice is called *serac* or *glacier ice*. Yet another type of ice is known as *soft white ice*; it contains a large amount of trapped air and is often frothy.

Ice can also be formed by atmospheric conditions. *Rime ice* is a dull white deposit caused by the freezing of water droplets (condensation) on objects exposed to the wind. Deposits of this type of ice are always built up toward the wind. Rime ice occurs especially in humid mountain areas which are close to the sea—places such as the Cascades, the Southern Andes, and Scotland. *Hoarfrost* is different from rime in that it is caused by sublimation (evaporation) of water vapor from the air onto solid objects. When hoarfrost occurs on a snow surface, it is called *surface hoar*. This commonly develops on clear cold nights when strong radiation and conduction carry away the heat of sublimation from the snow. I saw this surface hoar appear every night that I spent on the snowfields of Mount Kenya; it was due to the very cold nights and warm days. In the mornings I had to climb with gloves because the razor-sharp surface-hoar crystals would quickly have shredded my unprotected knuckles.

When solar radiation penetrates the surface snow layer and causes melting just below the surface at the same time that freezing conditions occur at the surface, *firnspiegel* or *firn mirror*, results. When it develops on steep snow slopes, this thin layer of clear ice can make for peculiar climbing conditions. I once found some on the north face of Mount Fay in Canada; though the steepest pitch was nearly 80 degrees and hard white ice, it was relatively easy to climb because I could break through the *firnspiegel* here and there and find perfect little pockets and "letter boxes" for my hands and feet.

Crampon points will barely penetrate the surface of *hard ice*, also called *water-ice*, *gully ice*, and *live ice*. Its hardness, plasticity, and brittleness will vary with age, temperature, and the amount of air contained within. *Hard white ice* is white and opaque, with many distinct air bubbles. It is usually new ice and is often layered and brittle. Frozen waterfalls are often composed of hard white ice. The key to finding good conditions for climbing these waterfalls is to pick a day that is not too warm for the ice to melt but not so cold that the ice is brittle.

Brittle ice is usually new, young ice deposited after a rain or formed on the surface by the daily thaw-and-freeze cycle. Often this brittle ice is only a few inches thick on the surface and clearing it away will expose a more workable medium.

Green ice is a clear water-ice with few air bubbles. It will vary in hardness and color until it becomes very clear, dense, and hard. In places such as Alaska and Antarctica, where extreme temperatures speed up the aging process, this ice will take on a bluish color. *Blue ice* and *green ice*, however, cannot be differentiated with exactitude. *Black ice* is very old gully ice mixed with dirt and gravel; it is extremely tough, like reinforced concrete. To hit this ice with the pick of the axe is like hitting plastic; it leaves only a small gouge and the pick has a tendency to stick. Chopping steps in black ice is quite difficult, but thankfully it is rarely found.

Verglas is thin water-ice on top of rock. It is formed by rain or meltwater freezing onto the rock. Sometimes a freezing rain will occur and supercooled raindrops can instantly freeze onto the rock. This often forms a veneer of ice, making for the most difficult climbing conditions of all, for crampons won't stick in the thin and nearly invisible ice, and rubber-soled shoes won't grip either. One of the most impressive and sobering photographs I've ever seen is of two German climbers who were caught in a chimney during a freezing rain. The photo shows two bodies frozen behind a foot of ice.

On ice we are not only concerned with color but also with the lack of it. Opaqueness denotes softness, color indicates hardness, clarity equals brittleness, cracks and fractures should mean weaknesses— or it can be the *opposite* of these! Only experience can begin to teach the subtleties of ice.

In addition to the physical composition of the various types of ice, another characteristic of the medium concerns its steepness. I have read many accounts in alpine journals where climbers are doing battle with 60- and 70-degree pitches of black ice. More often than not, these climbs are usually not over 50 degrees and are usually hard snow or soft ice. Even the angle of the Walker Spur on the Grandes Jorasses is only 50 degrees! Look closely at photos of ice climbing (not in this book, of course!) and you will notice that very often they have been taken with the camera tilted to make the slope look steeper. It's difficult to make pitches of snow and ice look steep because they rarely are steep.

The big snow and ice faces in the Alps average from 45 to 55 degrees. Gullies of *live ice* can be steeper and, of course, frozen waterfalls can be vertical. If you are going by a guidebook or someone's assessment of the angle of a slope, you can usually knock off 10 degrees for a more realistic estimate. For reasons of communication I will label a slope up to 30 degrees as *gentle*; 30 to 45 degrees is *moderate*; 45 to 60 degrees is *steep*; and 60 degrees and over will be called *extremely steep*. There is one more category of steepness that is in such popular usage that I will lump all sections from 80 to 90 degrees as *vertical*.

Crampons and the First Steps

Crampons are an extremely necessary piece of equipment for the ice climber. There are many types on the market nowadays: they can be hinged or rigid; adjustable or not; long-pointed or short-pointed; some have four points, but most have either ten or twelve. How can the neophyte ice climber begin to choose? Actually, it's quite easy. Buy a rigid twelve-point model with medium-length (32-millimeter) points. These factors are absolute prerequisities for learning the techniques described in this book. Whether or not the crampon is adjustable (a definite plus whenever you change boots) is not relevant to the techniques. A further discussion of crampons will be found in Chapter 4, since the nuances are more important for the "front-pointing" method of climbing ice.

Beginning ice climbers often ask me where to practice their cramponing techniques. I tell them that icefalls are to ice what boulders are to rockclimbing. These short cliffs are good places to develop your skills, and the semi-soft serac ice usually found there is a natural for French technique. In lieu of a good glacier, much can be learned on rock slabs and steep grass slopes. (I have had to use crampons more than once to negotiate a slippery grass slope!) When first trying out crampons, your immediate problem will be trying not to trip over yourself. You must keep your feet wider apart than you do in normal walking. You'll soon learn to avoid tearing socks, windpants, and gaiters (not to mention your leg) on these sharp new points. You'll also soon realize that the points are penetrating the snow vertically rather than being dragged horizontally. A shuffle won't do at all.

Walking about on the suncupped and unevenly frozen névé of a summer glacier is ideal for loosening the ankles before a climb. In the French method you must be able to flex your ankles easily, which is why the old French guides are so good at this technique. They have strained and stretched the ligaments in their ankles so many times over the years (bad knees and loose ankles are old climbers' diseases) that keeping their feet flat on a 50-degree ice slope is natural. If your boots are high and stiff, or just new and unflexed, don't lace them up all the way at first.

French crampon technique is strikingly similar to pure friction climbing on rock slabs. The footwork and body movements are identical. Imagine ascending a smooth rock slab that gradually steepens. The progression would go like this: (1) walk directly up; (2) splay your feet apart at about 90 degrees; (3) turn your hands sideways with feet pointed forward—the climbing is oblique with the inside arm keeping the body in balance and away from the

Pied à plat: *French crampon technique is strikingly similar to pure friction climbing on rock slabs.*

63

High up in the Diamond Couloir on Mount Kenya. Mike Covington Photo.

rock; (4) point your feet down and face your body increasingly outward until at the limit of adhesion you are almost backing up the rock; (5) finally you must face the rock and use small footholds for the toe of the boot. The common denominator of the first four stages is that the feet are flat on the rock; only at the last does edging on the toes (front-pointing) become necessary.

The use of crampons and ice axe for support allows you to climb much steeper slopes than you can friction climb. Balance and adhesion are the keys to ice climbing. Just as in pure friction climbing, adhesion comes from keeping as much of the surface area of the feet as possible in contact with the rock or ice; balance comes from keeping the weight directly over the feet.

Upward Progression

Using the same steps of friction-slab progression mentioned earlier, imagine climbing a gradually steepening slope of frozen

Page 65, Doug Tompkins on Hell's Lum
Crag, Cairngorms, Scotland.

Page 66, John Cunningham on Ben Nevis,
Scotland. Rob Taylor Photo.

Page 67, Jim Kanzler on Emperor Face,
Mount Robson, Canadian Rockies. Pat Callis
Photo.

Page 68, "Fallen Angel," Waterton Lakes
National Park, Canada.

Page 69, The author, Waterton Lakes
National Park, Canada. Rob Taylor Photo.

Pages 70-71, First pitch of Green Gully near
Bozeman, Montana. Lindalee Kanzler
Photo.

Page 72. Rob Taylor in the Hemsedal Valley,
Norway. Henry Barber Photo.

snow. (1) On the gentle slope walk straight up carrying the ice axe like a walking stick or cane (*piolet canne*). (2) As the slope steepens, the feet naturally splay out like a duck's feet (*en canard*). (3) Still steeper, turn and climb diagonally up the slope, remembering to keep the axe uphill. When you change directions, switch the axe to the other hand. (This is where an ice axe keeper strap encourages poor technique.) As footing becomes more exacting, a more positive support is needed, and the axe shifts to the elegant cross-body *piolet ramasse*. (4) As the terrain steepens further, shift your axe again to the more positive grip of *piolet ancre*. On the ever-steepening ice, face your legs increasingly outward in order to stay flat. At the extreme, before resorting to front-pointing, your outside foot should be up behind you, pointing straight down; you will be almost sitting on it as you move the axe higher. This is *pied assis*. The more difficult techniques will be described below in detail. The accompanying photographs should also be carefully studied.

In *piolet ramasse* the axe is held nearly horizontal across the waist, with the pick pointed in the direction you are going. One hand is on the head, and the other is just above the ferrule. A common mistake is to hold the axe too vertically, with the head of the axe up by the shoulders. This encourages leaning in toward the ice, destroying balance. If you find yourself in this compromising position, relax your shoulders, drop your arms so the axe falls back horizontally across your waist, exhale, relax your mind, and begin again. A very good reason for a 70-centimeter axe is now apparent, for it just reaches the ice as you stand in balance on a moderate slope. The hand on the ferrule pushes down on the spike, which is wide and flat like a crampon point; the widest area pushes down on the snow. The feet are parallel on gentle slopes, but when the slope steepens, point the bottom foot downward; this rests the ankle by bending it in an easier direction. All the crampon points are in contact with the slope and present their widest profile in case the snow is soft. Just as in friction climbing, use is made of any irregularities in the slope. The knees are bent away from the slope, kept apart, and the body weight is kept directly over the feet. The axe is moved upward and planted while in the "position of balance," with the outside leg below and behind the inside.

Actually getting your feet to flatten on the slope will be a problem. Make sure your boots are flexible enough in the ankle. While stepping upward, the ankle should be relaxed and the foot loose. Stepping onto the slope the uphill points will naturally touch first. If your ankle is relaxed at that instant, the foot will roll outward,

Pied marche, piolet canne. *Tom Frost Photo.*

Piolet ramasse *on a moderately angled slope. The climber is in balance, the axe has just been planted higher, but before the next step is taken, the upper ankle must roll down so that all the crampon points are secure in the ice.* Tom Frost Photo.

Climbing Ice: The French Method

Changing directions. Tom Frost Photos.

pivoting on the upper crampon points until the lower points bite the ice. You are now on a stable platform and your ankle has reached its necessary flex with a little stretching but no straining. After all, remember that *piolet ramasse* was developed to conserve energy.

To change directions, begin from the balance position by bringing the outside foot up to roughly the same height as the inside foot; the toe is pointed *slightly uphill*. Then turn the inside foot in the other direction. Reverse the grip on the axe, then bring the outside foot through to a new position of balance. Re-plant the axe and continue in the new direction.

As the angle increases from moderate to steep, *pied à plat* footwork continues to work comfortably, but moving up using just the spike for support begins to feel precarious, and one casts around for more positive security. The obvious solution is to swing the pick into the snow, grab the top of the head with the other hand, thumb under the adze, then step up to a new position of balance and reset the axe. This is *piolet ancre*, literally, "ice-axe anchor." Sometimes several steps can be taken as you climb up past the handle of the axe before it gets too low for balance.

The axe has now changed from a balance aid to a positive pull hold, and the properties of the pick that help it to hold well in a wide range of ice conditions now become important. Many modern axes have developed into grotesque forms that make them more suitable for assassination than for climbing ice. Swinging a properly designed axe, notice that the droop of the pick coincides with the arc of the swing; it thus enters the ice with the least disturbance. Once set, the curved design helps hold the axe in position. Older designs are not curved enough and tend to pop out as soon as downward weight is applied.

The curved pick also has a cutting edge on top, a sharp chisel tip, and several deep notches under the pick which further help lock it in place. The difficulty most climbers have with *piolet ancre* is overcoming an awkward, wobbly swing; aiming for a particular spot will help keep the wobble effect minimal.

A second, more subtle, problem is knowing just what direction to pull on the axe once it is set. After setting the pick it seems reasonable to drop the shaft until the spike rests on the ice. After all, two points of support are more stable than one, right? But this actually loosens the pick in its hole and disengages the teeth, popping the axe out in spite of its excellent droop. The exact opposite is correct. A gentle and constant *outward* pull on the ferrule sets the teeth and locks the pick in place. When climbing up past the shaft of the axe until you are above it, don't forget that pushing down on the head has the same loosening effect as dropping the spike onto the ice. Keeping the shaft away from the ice also keeps your body in balance by keeping it from leaning in. To remove the axe, just push down on the handle and out it comes.

The steeper the slope, the more the toes point downhill, and the more the ankles must be bent. The body also begins to face away from the slope. On extremely steep snow you are almost backing

Climbing with piolet ancre. *The next step is to remove the axe while in the balance position; then plant it higher and to the front.*

Below, the master French alpinist, André Contamine demonstrates piolet ancre; *note how the shaft of the axe is kept away from the slope for better balance and ease of removal.*

Climbing Ice: The French Method

A demonstration of piolet ancre. *Rob Taylor Photos.*

Climbing Ice: The French Method

up. When it becomes so steep that it is difficult to pass the inside foot between the slope and the outside leg, progress can be made by small steps. Keep the upper foot above, the lower foot below, and do not cross them. Here it may be necessary to plant the axe with each step. There is a natural tendency for beginners to shuffle their feet like this even on moderate slopes, but this is a bad habit because it's slow and tends to make the climber forget about proper balance.

If you have trouble keeping in balance while moving the axe up, push the body away from the slope, face more outward, and spread the knees wide apart, bending them outward.

On extremely steep slopes you increasingly run into the problem of keeping your balance while you take out the ice axe to move it higher. An extra step, called *pied assis*, can be added to the normal one-two-three *piolet ancre* sequence; this places the body in a more secure attitude. (1) From a balance position plant the axe *piolet ancre* as high as possible. (2) Move your outside foot up and forward (further up and less forward than in normal *piolet ancre*). (3) Bring up the inside foot as usual. (4) Plant your outside foot under your buttocks, toes pointing straight down. You then "sit down" like sitting in your étriers on artificial climbs. This contortionist act should put you in balance so that the axe can be taken out and re-planted. Notice that the body arches to stay in balance against steepness or to snake over bulges.

Descending Ice

Returning to the example of pure friction climbing, notice that keeping your feet *flat* is once again the key. In descending a steadily steepening rock slab the progression would go like this: (1) Walk directly down (*pied marche*); (2) Place the feet at 90 degrees to each other (*pied en canard*), bend and spread apart the knees, lean the body forward; (3) Turn the body sideways, keeping the feet pointed diagonally down (*pied à plat*); (4) Face in, toe down, and use small holds (*front-pointing*).

Try this on a slope of frozen névé. *Piolet canne, pied marche*: proper technique demands that the axe be planted as far forward as possible, thereby putting the body weight directly over the feet. The feet point straight down on gentle slopes and are *en canard* on moderate slopes. On steeper slopes use *piolet ramasse*: this is essentially the classic glissading position except that the spike is thrust in and the axe is used for support while the feet are moved down.

Lean far forward for proper balance, and grip the shaft close to the surface of the snow. As the slope steepens further, two more techniques come into play. First is *piolet appui*. *Appui* means support and this technique does just that; it gives momentary support when descending short steep sections on rough terrain. The pick is not planted but just rests while the spike is placed on the snow. Next is *piolet rampe*: the pick is planted as far below as possible, in an upside-down *ancre*, and is used as a bannister for support. Crampon down, sliding your hand along the shaft, and *pulling slightly out* until the head is behind you. Pull out the pick and replace the axe below. Remember to keep the knees bent and spread wide apart, the feet *en canard*, and the body as far forward as possible. This requires a degree of boldness to do well. Only pulling

Andre Contamine in piolet appui/pied à plat *on serac ice, and Malinda Chouinard doing the same on a rock slab.*

Climbing Ice: The French Method

outward on the shaft will keep you in balance. It is rather like turning into the fall line when skiing a steep slope—to hesitate and sit back is to invite disaster. Given perfect conditions, short slopes of over 70 degrees can be descended in this manner.

As on rock, when it becomes too steep to descend facing outward, you turn sideways. Facing in should be the last resort. The sideways technique for descending such steep terrain is *piolet ancre*. The method is the same as on the ascent, only reversed. The problem is in lodging the axe, designed as it is for a full arm swing, as low as possible. Instead of cramping your swing, try setting it out horizontally to the side, then diagonal down rotating the shaft as you pass underneath.

Most beginners will find the French ascending and descending techniques very tiring on the thighs, legs, and ankles. This is because they have not yet developed a dynamic rhythm. They constantly stop in the middle of a step with all their weight on one leg. They are usually off balance, so they must hold on to the axe even more tightly, which puts them ever more out of balance, etc. Even walking down the street would be very tiring if we were to stop and stand on one leg for a moment before each stride. But the act of walking, or climbing, is effortless because of *rhythm*.

Most people can learn to do *piolet ramasse* or front-pointing techniques, but that in itself is nothing. What makes them climbers is the rhythmic linking together of these individual moves. Oozing through a difficult icefall requires changing techniques every few meters to adjust to conditions and terrain. The smooth linking of all these techniques is the art of climbing ice. Only practice gives the skill, balance, and confidence that will make French technique effortless and sure.

Opposite, using piolet ramasse/pied en canard *to descend a short ice bulge.*

The sequence at the right shows piolet rampe. *Note that long steps are taken and the upper body leans into the fall line for proper balance. To further save time, the axe is not replaced until the hand is all the way down the head. Tom Frost Photos.*

81

Dennis Hennek, Mount Mendel

December is usually pretty late in the year to be going into the Sierra without skis, but there had been only one big storm so far and that had been back in October. The going on the hard snow up to Lamarck Col was really easy, and we got there in the early afternoon. From the Col we could look straight across into the couloir on Mount Mendel, and right off we could see why it had never been done in full-on ice conditions. Nothing is worse than looking at an ice gully straight on!

Dennis Hennek and I dropped down into the basin and found a cave to set up our bivouac sack. We had a nervous night thinking about the climb and felt very remote and strung out. The dawn came up over the White Mountains in technicolor, and in an hour it was snowing lightly. We kicked steps up the lower slopes, which I was sure must be ice in October. When it got steeper, we stuck close by the rock so we could get chock belays.

Higher up we found powder snow on top of dark, dirty ice. I tried to chop a step, but even though I swung the axe with both hands it made only a nick. It was like trying to chop into an asphalt road. That was only the second time I had ever seen real black ice. I figured that since it was only about 45 degrees that it would be easier to front-point it instead of trying to chop steps. I put in a good runner above me on the rock and finger-tipped across with my hands on the rock and feet on the ice. Later, I got out into the main gully where the ice was green, and although it was getting on to 55 degrees, the stuff was climbable. The ice axe seemed to be holding OK, but the ice piton that I was using for a dagger was just worthless; we hadn't got into ice hammers yet in 1965. I was standing on my front points about 20 meters out where the gully steepens to over 60 degrees. The pick of my axe was barely in because I couldn't get a good swing. It was so steep and I couldn't trust that wretched dagger to hold me in balance.

So there I was locked on, unable to move up or down and my legs were crapping out. It was snowing hard by now and spindrift avalanches were coming down in waves. A good-sized slide came down and began to build between me and the ice. I couldn't lean out to let it pass because my balance was so precarious. There was one point when you could have knocked me over with a straw. Don't ask me how, but I got out of there and onto the rock, where I put in a chock and rappelled.

That night it snowed half a meter, and in the morning we had a horrible talus slope to fight back up to the Col. It took us close to three hours, mostly on our hands and feet, to go 200 meters. Dennis lost his ice axe, and I almost broke my leg a hundred times in those boulders. The thing that kept me going was thinking about how I was going to go back to the shop and forge a hammer with a long, thin pick with teeth on it for climbing ice. No more of this ice dagger bullshit for me.

4
Climbing Ice: The Front-Point Method

Front-pointing

As mentioned in Chapter 1, it was the German and Austrian mountaineers of the Eastern Alps who first used the technique whereby only the front points of the crampon were in contact with the ice. The harder snow and ice of that particular region was a prime cause of this radical development.

As ice becomes more dense, it also becomes harder, and the necessity to spread weight out over many crampon points of support as a means of treading delicately is replaced by an impression of the sheer difficulty of penetrating it at all. So we unkink our strong-but-supple French ankles, uncoil the knees back from their sideways-to-backward orientation, and turn to face the ice.

While French technique faces increasingly away from the ice with steepness, the front-pointer finds the ice staring him more and more in the face. The front-pointer, too, is a balance climber and must never forget it, but his position offers several advantages. The sidelong, flexed-ankle kick of the French method reminds me of a soccer player working for control. On the other hand, the front-pointer's vigorous kick into the ice can be compared to the soccer

Opposite, "On steep ice you must place your concentration on the tips of your crampons and never let it wander from them!"

Climbing Ice: The Front-Point Method

player's long down-the-field kick. But do not be fooled that greater force applied at fewer points from a position of mechanical advantage will alone secure attachment. As the ice gets colder and harder, it gets increasingly brittle as well, which means that the force of either hand or foot must be accurately applied to the ice to prevent shattering and cone breakouts. The face-on approach allows both arms and legs a natural swinging position, but many aspiring climbers are not accustomed to swinging tools—the axe, hammer, and place kick. It helps to have a background in carpentry and to be ambidextrous.

Tom Frost Photo

When I speak about front points or front-pointing technique, I don't refer to just those two horizontal points that stick out from the end of your crampon. Proper technique demands that all *four* forward points be used: that is, the two front points and the two vertical points just behind. Stand with your heels low and all four points in the ice, the back two making a little platform to aid stability and provide more surface area so the front points don't shear through rotten ice or soft snow. Keeping your heels low relaxes the muscles in your legs. Try standing on just the two front points with your feet horizontal, then raise your heels and feel the strain in your calves and notice how the points want to shear out. Now drop your heels and feel your leg muscles relax and your whole position stabilize. On blue ice the front points must be placed with one sharp, swift kick. A wavering blow causes vibration which tends to shatter the ice rather than making a clean, sharp hole. Any motion after the points are set can dislodge them. After the axe is in solidly you can move your feet up by a technique Cunningham calls a "little jog-hop." When done smoothly, this dynamic flurry of three little hops will firmly plant the front points with less effort than doing it by the numbers.

The Tools

Climbing hard brittle ice is the most demanding use of the pick on an axe or alpine hammer. Besides a proper droop to correspond to the radius of its swing, each has a thin, sharp pick for easy penetration. The thinner the pick, the more curve, and the deeper the teeth, the more the pick will stick in the ice. Of course this emphasis on clawing efficiency yields a pick that can be embarrassingly sticky to cut steps with, but then it's nice to have done away with all that hacking when we can get away without it.

Another advantage of the 70-centimeter axe is noticed on steep, hard ice: namely, that it is close to the balanced length for swinging its head weight. The oval-shaped shaft makes for a less wobbly, more accurate, straight swing. The full-width shaft down to the ferrule gives a more secure grip than a tapered shaft.

Front-pointing brings out the best qualities of rigid crampons, which hold tightly to the boot soles and make accurate placements possible on the ice. The rigidity and lack of hinge dampen vibration and help keep the crampon in the ice; the stiffness, in conjunction with a stiff boot sole, delays fatigue in the ankle and calf. The front points of the crampon should be curved downward like the curved pick of an axe. Beware of front points that are too far apart, for unless your front-pointing technique is perfect, with feet always exactly at right angles to the ice, you will find yourself standing on only one point.

To be able to crampon up hard, steep ice, you must have stiff-soled boots, rigid crampons, and a perfect fit. A soft-soled boot in combination with a hinged crampon is less than worthless for climbing ice. The front points must penetrate the hard ice and the primary cause of lack of penetration is vibration, which will cause the ice to shatter. Vibration itself can be caused by front points that are too dull, by points angled down instead of curved, by sloppy fit, by soft-soled boots, or by the play in the joint of a hinged crampon. A good, well-fitting crampon will be a part of your

Ruedi Homberger Photo.

You cannot learn to fly by flying. First you must learn to walk, and to run, and to climb, and to dance.

—Nietzsche

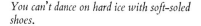

You can't dance on hard ice with soft-soled shoes.

Climbing Ice: The Front-Point Method

foot just as a well-fitting klettershoe is. A crampon fits well if it will stay on the boot without straps.

In recent years several new crampon designs have appeared on the market. One model has narrow, vertical front points which are great on hard ice but shear right through soft ice or snow. Another has all four front points raked forward, which is fine for front-pointing hard snow, but poor for hard ice and mixed climbing. There is even an attachment available which has upward-curving front points for overhanging ice! All these gimmicks are too specialized to be useful.

The French have developed a long-pointed snow crampon for their technique. The points are long, broad, and flat so as to gain maximum purchase on the relatively soft frozen névé of the French Alps. They are excellent for the hard snow or soft ice conditions of the French Alps, New Zealand, or the Himalayas, but they are worthless on hard ice, where they act as miniature stilts. Conversely, the short-spike crampons which grew up on the harder ice of the Eastern Alps do not penetrate deep enough into snow or rotten ice; they also lack resistance to shearing. You should either pick the correct type of crampon for your area or settle for one with medium-length points.

Keep your crampon points sharp and avoid walking on rocks with them. I sharpen mine with a file before every climb. Don't use a grinder since it will overheat the metal and change its temper. Before every climb check the crampons and straps thoroughly for any weaknesses or cracks. On adjustable crampons check to see that the screws are tight.

Soft, sticky snow "balling" in the crampon points produces extra weight and slipperiness that can be annoying and dangerous. The logical solution is to take the crampons off, since snow that soft will rarely require more purchase than step-kicking or heeling down will give. Occasionally slush will hide a slippery ice base, a condition both demanding crampons and hopelessly balling them. Scooting your feet forward with each step will help clear the snow from rigid crampons which have all the side points aligned. Another solution is to wrap plastic tape or a layer of coated nylon cloth over the crampon points. This keeps the wet snow from sticking to the metal framework but is not meant to substitute for removing the crampons when they are no longer needed.

Some sort of hammer is nearly always carried on any ice climb. An Alpine hammer can be used for placing ice pitons, testing or placing rock pitons, removing chocks, and clearing dirt and moss out of cracks. The North Wall hammer is actually a short (50–55

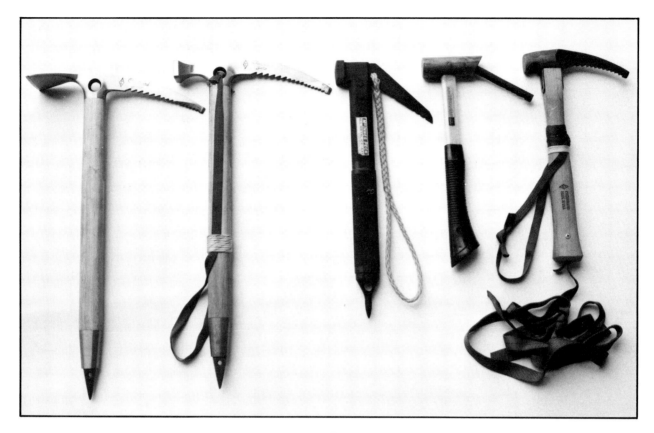

Piolet *North Wall Hammer* *Terrordactyl* *Hummingbird* *Alpine Hammer*

centimeters) ice axe with a hammer head rather than an adze. This tool has been in use for almost forty years by Austrian and German ice climbers. It is used like an Alpine hammer, but its shaft functions like an ice axe shaft. A Scottish invention called the Terrordactyl has an inclined rather than curved pick. It works particularly well for climbing rotten, hollow ice because it is not so dependent on the teeth being stuck in for security as in most curved gear.

The "Hummingbird" has a pick inclined like that of the Terrordactyl, but it's formed out of tubing so there is less displacement on brittle ice. Its special use is for climbing winter waterfalls.

Most of these tools are carried in hammer holsters on the belt (converts to clean climbing will be pleased to note that their holsters are still good for something!).

So what tool do we use? I'll tell you my preference at this moment, but remember that every climber has his own style and that techniques are continually changing. Most any combination of tools can be made to do the job, provided that you have sorted out your technique. On a typical Alpine face, say the north face of the

Climbing Ice: The Front-Point Method

Triolet in hard snow conditions with some patches of ice, I'd carry only a 70-centimeter axe. If I were soloing, or if the face were a solid sheet of hard, 55-degree ice, then I would use a North Wall hammer and an axe together quite a bit.

For Scottish gullies, or for climbing vertical waterfalls, I would use a Model Zero ice axe of 50- or 55-centimeter length in combination with the Model Zero North Wall hammer. The technique would be pure front-pointing with *piolet traction* (*traksyõ*), a technique which will be discussed later. Remember, whatever tool you have in your hand is also your belay should your feet slip out, so place it swiftly and surely. Aim for an imaginary X on the ice. This will guide your blow and make a more positive and less wobbly swing. Experience will enable you to detect small weaknesses in the ice where the pick will seat best.

Upward Progression

The simplest use of front-pointing, one you may run into on approaches and in glacier climbing, is in getting up short, steep sections. Suppose you are trucking along on a gentle slope in the normal *pied marche* position and you are confronted with a steep bulge. Without breaking your stride and pace, change your axe from *piolet canne* into *piolet panne* position. To do this, just drop the pick forward to hit the ice, hand still on top of the head, and walk up on your front points, keeping the heels low. With the axe as an extra aid to balance, a little flurry of front-pointing will preserve your momentum and carry you over the bulge.

When the pace of *piolet panne* slows down to having to move the limbs "by the numbers," the reason is invariably steepness; steeper ground requires more balance. So it is only reasonable and natural to move the tools above the shoulders. (You lift your arms on steep rock without even thinking of it.) The axe is held by the head like a dagger and is stabbed into the snow. This method, called *piolet poignard* (*pwàñàr*), works very well on steep slopes where the frozen snow is still soft enough for the pick of the axe to penetrate without making it necessary to swing it from the shaft. *Piolet poignard* can be used all the way up climbs in Scotland and the Western Alps, where conditions soft enough for it are often found.

When the snow or ice is too hard and/or too steep to use *piolet poignard*, switch to *piolet ancre*. Face the slope, standing on normal front points, and swing the pick in as high as possible above you. Front-point up, moving the hands up the handle and finally onto the head in the classic *piolet ancre* position. Continue front-pointing until the axe is waist high, or *piolet panne*, before moving it higher.

Above, place it swiftly and surely. Rob Taylor Photo.
Opposite, the late Tom Patey using double piolet panne. A very quick way to "run" up moderate slopes on all fours. John Cleare Photo.
Below, piolet poignard with the left hand. Tom Frost Photo.

Climbing Ice: The Front-Point Method

Piolet ancre. *Front-pointing evolves into*
piolet panne. *The axe was planted only*
once to surmount this bulge. Rob Taylor
Photos.

Climbing Ice: The Front-Point Method

It soon becomes obvious that a longer axe can be placed higher, letting you front-point up more steps before replacing the axe; this saves time and effort. Of course the advantage is lost on extremely steep slopes if the axe becomes unwieldy by being too long and badly balanced.

It takes only a little experimenting to realize that on a given square meter of ice it will make a tremendous difference where you plant the pick of the axe. Sometimes the ice can be so brittle that many blows are spent before a solid placement is found. Look for differences in color in the ice. Sometimes a streak of urine-colored ice on a brittle, frozen waterfall will be softer and offer superb pick placements.

As the terrain becomes extremely steep, the *piolet ancre* in combination with front-pointing will not work because the climber is unable to take out the axe and move it higher for fear of losing balance. This is the terrain where tools are used in each hand. When it is this steep, you must have three points of support in at all times. As on steep rock, the legs pushing upward are the major support, but the arms must carry some of the weight. Needless to say, each of the three points of support must be solid enough to hold the full body weight should the others come out. Actually pulling up on the tools is known as *piolet traction*.

The best foot technique on extremely steep ice is normal front-pointing, but the crampon points that were curved downward for effective setting on lower angles will now glance off the ice if the heels are held high at all. The steeper the ice, the more a conscious effort must be made to keep the heels low. A common mistake is to make long reaches and in so doing unconsciously raise the heels, shearing out the front points. Be particularly careful pulling up over the top of a vertical section. Your body may be leaning over, but your legs are still on the vertical. Whenever you are front-pointing, keep your feet straight into the ice, not in the least splayed out like you normally stand. Splaying your feet out will leave you standing only on the inside points. The outside front points on certain crampons are purposely made longer to help correct this fault. On steep ice you must concentrate your attention on the tips of your crampons and *never let it wander from there!*

Anyone who has done much front-pointing knows how fatiguing it is in the thighs and calves. Stiff-soled boots with rigid crampons; heels down; dynamic yet relaxed technique; all these will delay fatigue, but there is a much more ingenious solution called *pied troisième* (*trwàzyèm*) that blends the *pied à plat* with *front-pointing* footwork. Just front-point with one foot and rest the other by

Above, Big Bill March on the Cascade in the Cairngorms in 1968—the first time piolet traction *was used in Scotland. Opposite, be particularly careful to keep your heels low when pulling over the top of a bulge. John Cunningham Photo. Below,* pied troisième. *Doug Robinson Photo.*

95   *Climbing Ice: The Front-Point Method*

The author using pied troisième *as a rest step on hard ice. Tom Frost Photo.*

turning it out sideways and relaxing the ankle in *pied à plat*. When you get tired of front-pointing on one foot, switch over to your other foot. This technique is a far less tiring method of climbing steep ice than front-pointing, and it is certainly easier to learn than pure French technique. It can also relieve the awkwardness of pointing the feet in the opposite directions at the end of a zig or a zag in the *pied à plat*. *Pied troisième* (the name comes from the third position of ballet) means literally "third foot," but think of it as "3 o'clock," the position of the feet when done correctly. For the average climber this technique, used in combination with *piolet ancre* for the hands, should be the most valuable of all the cramponing methods we have discussed. It works on snow or ice and on all slopes from moderate to extremely steep. You need not be in super condition to do it even on long, arduous climbs.

Probably the fastest, most efficient method of climbing a steep ice slope is by front-pointing using a 70-centimeter axe in *piolet ancre*. Place the axe in as high above as possible and go up three or four steps on the front points. Then use a *pied troisième* as the position of balance, or rest step so you can move the axe higher.

Vertical and Overhanging Ice

You will have more trouble holding onto the hand tools the steeper it gets until under an overhang most of your weight will be on your arms. Arm strength is a limiting factor in climbing vertical ice, just as it is in climbing strenuous hand jams or overhanging face climbing. The arms must be kept straight and not bent at the elbows, so that as little strain as possible is put on the biceps. Hang from bone, not muscle. To minimize gripping the tools so tightly that the forearms get tired, use gloves with non-slip palms and use *wrist loops.*

There are all sorts of methods for tying wrist loops onto the tools, and I will describe only the methods that I prefer. The important thing is to have the hand tied onto the tool at the balance position just above the ferrule and to have the strain in line with the shaft. The long leash that I occasionally use on my ice axe is half-hitched into the hole on the head and is of the correct length so that I can put a hitch just above the balance position on the shaft. This keeps my hand locked onto the shaft for the occasional vertical section or for a long bout of step-cutting.

For serious waterfall climbing I keep wrist loops permanently tied onto my tools. I use a sling of 10-millimeter webbing, thread it through the hole, and then tie or sew it into a loop that extends to about the end of the spike. Then I whip it securely onto the shaft just above the balance point. The loop which is left must be long enough to accept a gloved hand. My hand goes into the loop from below, does a twist, and grabs the shaft. If I am not wearing gloves, then two or three twists can be made to take up the slack. This system gives a secure grip onto the shaft yet allows your hand to get in and out of the wrist loop quickly.

Just because a section of ice is overhanging doesn't mean that you must resort to artificial aid. But before you go out on a limb on this irreversible pitch you had better make sure that your technique and equipment are well sorted out. Apply the same rules for holding the tools and for front-pointing as on extremely steep angles, but more so. At no time will you be in balance, and even more of your body weight will be supported by your arms.

The tools are planted as high as possible but off to the side so that you don't knock blocks of ice on your head (and should a tool pop out it won't hit you in the face!). When you can get away with it, put only one tool in "bombproof;" the other is placed with less vigor. This allows you to remove the latter tool more easily in order to quickly plant it higher.

Free climbing on overhanging ice.

A wrist loop.

97　　*Climbing Ice: The Front-Point Method*

After planting the tools avoid gripping the shafts tightly; rather, hang from the wrist loops to save strength. Remember also to maintain a slight outward pull on the tools to prevent the teeth from unsetting. This also keeps your body away from the ice so that you can more easily keep your heels low. Both feet are kept at

the same level before you move the hand tools higher. Also, the feet are kept wide apart to create a more stable base. With proper technique the body forms an X. Never move higher on your axes than nose height. Resting is done by planting both axes bombproof and hanging out from the wrist loops on fully extended arms.

The two photos on these pages illustrate proper technique on overhangs.

Above, traversing technique.
Below, double-axe technique.

Finally, for overcoming vertical and overhanging cornices and bergschrunds there is the *double axe* technique. You merely use two axes in the *piolet manche* attitude and alternately drive them in, kicking steps for the feet.

Traverses and Descents

Traverses on extremely steep or vertical ice are best made by *piolet traction*. When the ice is hard and brittle, avoid rotating or moving the axe after it is placed. To effect a traverse, plant the trailing axe at a 45-degree angle as close to the body as possible, then lean off

this axe to place the leading tool as far forward as possible, making sure the shaft hangs down vertically. Shift your weight onto this tool and replace the trailing axe. Footwork is by the front-pointing method—either shuffle or cross over the feet. In either case avoid the tendency to splay the feet.

Front-pointing or *pied troisième* works very well for *descending steep ice*. One merely reverses the ascending techniques. As on rock, going down is harder than going up. Avoid the tendency to step down too far or trying to set the crampon points with the heels too high. When trying to set the axe low, you will soon notice the difficulty of swinging a proper arc with less than a full arm swing.

Climbing Ice: The Front-Point Method

It usually helps to descend diagonally by planting the axe slightly off to the side.

The tools and climbing techniques discussed in this section will enable you to climb vertical and even overhanging blue ice. The limits of front-pointing are defined by the steepness and hardness of the ice and by the stamina and courage of the climber. However, these limits are boundless and can be pushed by physical conditioning, exact technique, and a confident attitude.

Mike Covington, high on the Diamond Glacier, Mount Kenya, climbs on his own style and uses a perfect blend of several techniques. Opposite, Dale Bard and Rob Taylor on a free ascent of the Middle Ice Fall of Mount Fay in the Canadian Rockies. The last six meters actually overhang about fifteen degrees.

Mount Mendel, Dennis Hennek Photo

I returned to Mount Mendel a few years later with Dean Moore. This time the couloir was a solid sheet of green ice for 350 meters, but now we had Alpine hammers, Climaxes, and the latest "Wart Hogs."

It didn't take us long to realize that the ice was awfully brittle. Sometimes the hammer would stick better and sometimes the axe. Usually we had to make sure the first blow would stick; otherwise the ice would be too shattered to try again. Often we had to clear off all the brittle junk for about ten or fifteen centimeters, and then get the pick into the more plastic ice underneath. It seemed that whenever we thought we had the right combination the ice would change.

After a while we got pretty good at telling what was ahead and could avoid the really brittle ice by moving a meter or so over to where it was slightly more opaque and softer. The biggest help was finding hairline fractures. If we aimed at one of those little cracks, the pick would go right in and stick every time. We just went from crack to crack, and about the time we were really pleased with ourselves for having found the "final solution," we got onto the 60-degree bulge that had given me so much trouble a few years before.

Well, I just couldn't get a damn thing in. Whenever I tried to slam in a hammer or Climaxe, it would break off a big, conical slab that would skid down onto my ankles and almost knock me off my front points. That's when I psyched out and started cutting steps.

Tom Frost Photo

105

5
Step-Cutting and Other Techniques

Step-cutting

During the past few years I have taught ice climbing to over four hundred persons. Many of them were experienced ice climbers; some were mountain guides. Yet I never found one person who knew even the rudiments of step-cutting. The skill, experience, and strength that is necessary to cut good steps has been replaced by technology. Even though proper crampon technique virtually eliminates the need to ever cut steps, there will be times when a thorough knowledge and proficiency with the axe will be worth more than the points of one's crampons. I maintain that a thorough knowledge of step-cutting is absolutely essential for promoting speed and efficiency in alpine climbing. There are many situations when you could be caught, whether by method or madness, without crampons when they could be useful. The alpine rambler or ski tourer might prefer to substitute skill with his axe for a kilo of crampons. On a mixed climb a well-wielded axe can save the crampons from jamming in chimneys and ventilating the water

Opposite, John Temple on delicate climbing in the icefall of the Coronation Glacier, Mount Stanley, Ruwenzori Range, Uganda. John Cleare Photo.

Step-Cutting and Other Techniques

Jim McCartney cutting pigeonhole steps on the Crab Crawl, Creag Meaghaidh. John Cleare Photo.

Chris Bonington cutting steps into the **Spider,** *on the Eiger in 1962. Ian Clough Photo*

bottles on the rest of the climb. A brief ice interlude might be bridged with steps sooner than crampons could be taken from the sack. And, while hurrying down by twilight, skill with the axe may save leaving it for a rappel anchor. Then there is the expeditionary situation where humping loads on front points is less than appealing. The guide with a novice client, or a weak or injured climber, would certainly appreciate his ability to chop steps. Only the person who has done a *grande course* knows the satisfaction of doing it with only the *piolet* as his companion.

The picks on modern ice axes have many diverse and specialized shapes. The pick designed for clawing will stick in the ice because of the teeth and the pointed end. A pick for cutting steps will have less curve, no teeth, and a wide chisel point. The better the pick works in *piolet ancre*, the worse it will be at step-cutting. A compromise shape will include a slightly curved pick with deep teeth and a fine chisel point. Using a certain amount of technique, this axe can be made to work adequately for all situations.

The recent changeover from shattering to clawing picks made it necessary that some other part of the ice axe serve for occasional step-cutting. The classic flat adze with sharp, square edges is an excellent tool for cutting steps in all but the hardest ice. Cupped adzes with rounded corners and gimmicks like serrated edges are all but worthless for anything except scooping ice cream.

Keep your ice axe sharp. The peasant working in the fields stops every hour to sharpen his hoe. So, too, does the expert ice man become sensitive to the dullness of his tools.

You will probably attack your first ice slope with strong muscles and feeble results. Considerable expertise is needed before you will be able to cut steps efficiently and with a minimum of effort. A long, arduous bout with a hard ice slope is usually necessary before you become proficient. After five hundred steps you begin to feel the importance of using well-directed, well-spaced blows and letting the weight of the axe do the work.

On low-angle slopes of firm snow it is possible to make a step with one blow of the axe and still maintain a normal uphill walking pace. More often it will take several blows. For ice, swing the axe in a near-vertical plane, using the inside corner of the adze. Make the first gouge at the near end of the step and make the next *away* from you. This way the adze doesn't stick and will remove more ice.

Hard ice demands cutting with the pick. To keep the pick from sticking in plastic ice, give an outward jerk on the shaft just as the pick is losing momentum in the ice. This will change its setting arc to a prying motion, which breaks out the ice instead of lodging the pick. Anyone who has tried to claw in brittle ice knows how a little wobble at the pick will shatter the ice rather than stick in it.

Hard, brittle ice, which tends to break out in conical plaques, demands a different cutting technique. First, direct a line of blows at right angles to a slope to make a fracture line base. Then chop above this line to carve out a step. The fracture line prevents the carving blows from breaking out the entire step. If you are not wearing crampons, make sure the steps slope inward. When you need to relax your legs, make the steps long enough to include the entire foot.

The normal pattern of steps is a *diagonal zigzag* up the slope. Angle up the slope as steeply as is comfortable, spacing the steps as far apart as possible without risking your balance. On a low-angle slope you need cut only one step and stand in it with one foot; the other just lies on the slope for balance. On steeper slopes you can either cut a step large enough for both feet or cut two steps each time before moving up, always staying in the balance position while cutting. To switch from a zig to a zag, cut a step for the

Two of the pitches we now encountered . . . were what is usually known as perpendicular, i.e., probably 70° to 75°, with small portions approaching 90°.

It was, of course, only due to the peculiar tough quality of the snow ice curtain hanging down these steeper portions that they were climbable at all. At angles such as these it is impossible to remain in toeholds in ice without holding on as well, and it is impossible to hoist the body up unless the handholds are cut so as to give a 'pull in.' These icy curtains allowed of this being done; frequently the pick broke through to soft snow or black vacancy, backed with green bulbs of ice, and 'pigeon-hole' holds resulted.

—*Harold Raeburn*
"A Scottish Ice Climb"
Scottish Mountaineering
Journal

Zigzag steps.

outside foot, and, before moving up, cut another step in the other direction.

If you are wearing crampons and wish to save time, you can make steps for the inside foot only and crampon across the gap with the outside foot. This is a good pattern for guides to use with clients.

On a steep slope it is usually faster to cut steps directly up the slope. Though more efficient, this *direct ascent* method is more tiring and is uncomfortable for the belayer, who is receiving all of the ice chips on his head. Generally, the steeper the angle, the further ahead the steps must be cut. Sometimes you may wish to cut mere toe steps or nicks, but to rest you should have an occasional flat, horizontal step.

A quick pattern for climbing up very steep ice (especially if you are wearing crampons) is to cut *mantleshelf steps*. Chop a long, horizontal step high above your head. The step should be long enough to allow room for both feet to be splayed out. If you are not wearing crampons, it helps to cut a handhold on one end of the step. Plant the ice axe up high for the other hand, pull up, and "mantleshelf" onto the step.

Vertical, and even overhanging, ice can be climbed with the help of *pigeonhole steps*. These are combined hand- and footholds, so the steps should be formed to make good jug holds yet be large enough for the foot. Since it becomes tiring for your legs to be in this essentially front-pointing position, you can make an occasional long, horizontal stance.

The fastest method of descent is by *ladder steps*. Standing sideways to the slope, cut a step directly below your feet and stand in it with your *outside* foot. Cut a second step slightly to the rear and as far below as you can reach; your *inside* foot steps down to this one. When stepping down, you do not cross your feet: outside foot goes forward, inside back. Keeping the steps staggered makes it easier to step down. On extremely steep slopes two steps need to be cut before you move down. The ice axe can be used in *piolet ancre* for support as you step down (or, faster yet, "palm" the upper step with your inside hand).

Mixed Climbing

Chris Jones wrote one of my favorite definitions of mixed climbing: "We were immediately slowed down as we struggled with a mixture of steep rock, ice, rotten rock covered by snow, snow mushrooms, general difficulty, and poor protection. I believe they call it 'mixed climbing.'"

*On the page opposite, the series of photos
shows mantleshelf steps, pigeonhole steps,
and ladder steps. Photos by Rob Taylor.
Left, mixed climbing. Doug Ross Photo.*

Mixed climbing is climbing on both ice and rock, either in quick
succession or actually at the same time. The principles of balance
and adhesion are still the basis of motion, but they are simultaneously applied to two different worlds with different rules where the
right hand must be wary of what the left foot is doing.

Besides blending two different modes of vertical motion, mixed
climbing means rockclimbing with crampons. This is done to save
the time of putting them on and taking them off and the risk of
doing the maneuver in an exposed or delicate situation. For instance, a hundred-foot fall that turned back an attempt of the
Eiger North Wall was caused by trying to take off crampons in too
precarious a position. With a well-fitting pair of crampons, the
points flush along the edge of the boot, climbing rock is not as

Step-Cutting and Other Techniques

difficult as it will at first feel. The first impression will be one of great remoteness. By standing on "little stilts" on the rock, all feel for its surface is gone from the sole of the foot. Yet edging on the points can be very precise. The habit, carried over from delicate face climbing, of keeping the foot stationary on the hold and in a fixed attitude even as the body moves by really pays off here. The little stilts will, of course, magnify any error such as raising the heel when stretching toward the next hold. Crampons are less able to adapt to this new position, whereas a rubber-soled boot will give a little by creeping along the rock. A crampon is more likely to pop.

Mixed climbing is thus a matter of blending and synthesizing techniques. It can be the most subtle of ice climbing arts, the natural progression beyond pure ice to *grand alpinisme*.

Artificial Climbing

Modern ice tools, *piolet traction*, and boldness should just about eliminate the need to ever rely on *artificial aids* in climbing ice. In reality, though, there is the odd exception to the rule; for instance, severely overhanging seracs or bergschrunds often cannot be climbed free.

The technique for climbing severe overhangs is identical to artificial climbing on rock. Place an ice piton as high as possible, clip in the rope and étriers, and climb up the rungs, taking tension if need be to place another peg higher. If the overhang isn't too great, you can stand only on your front points rather than étriers, using tension to stay in balance. Be careful here of putting too much of an outward pull on the ice piton when taking tension. Keep in mind also that an ice piton can melt out with body weight on it.

Another method that is much faster for climbing ice that is merely vertical or slightly overhanging uses the hand tools for anchors instead of ice pitons. It was discovered by Bugs McKeith and is in popular usage in Canada for climbing waterfalls. McKeith describes it: "It was on this climb [Weeping Wall] that we first used in earnest a technique unwittingly evolved through my own lack of boldness. On two previous occasions, faced by pillars of brittle, vertical ice, and lacking the guts to front point up them, I had attached aid slings to the shafts of both Terrordactyls and had found that, even on vertical ice, I could relax and spend as much time as I wished clearing rotten ice and placing each axe alternately to my complete satisfaction."

Above, Peter Farrell demonstrates artificial technique in New Zealand. Lynn Crawford Photo.
Opposite, mixed ground: The Hell's Lum Crag, Cairngorms.

During the late fifties and early sixties the impecunious British and American climbers in Chamonix stayed at the Biollay campsite. It was close to the train station, the center of town, and, of course, the Bar National. Though the camping was free, it was a desperate place to live. There were no toilet facilities or potable water, and when it rained (and of course that was the only time we were in camp) the place turned into a field of mud and stinking garbage. None of the French climbers would go near the place; most of them preferred the Hotel de Paris.

The daily routine was to sleep as late as possible, wolf down some porridge, and pad through the muck into town and the bakery. Afternoons were spent in the Bar National or, if it wasn't raining, sitting on park benches watching the un-approachable French birds walk by. Then it was back to the "Nash" for an evening of drinking. A stagger back to the Biollay woods completed the day's activities.

One morning, during a fifteen-day stretch of rain and snow, morale was at an all-time low. I was morosely walking over to get some water when I stopped in my tracks. A beautiful girl, stripped to her underwear, was washing in the stream. I could hardly believe my eyes, for the only women that hung around the Biollay in those days were usually as wretched as we were.

Since there was no avoiding at least a "good morning," we struck up a conver-sation. With a heavy Austrian accent she mentioned that she was here to climb but had been unable to find a partner. The next day dawned with blue skies, and off we went up to a hut. The following morning we set off for the Voie des Plaques on the Aiguille de Requin. The English guidebook deems it a classic and states that it's a good introduction to Alpine climbing. It's not difficult going (mainly low-angle slabs with an occasional section of Grade IV), but it is nearly a thousand meters long and involves a glacier approach. The French call this route the "Englishman's Bedroom" because so many British climbers come straight onto it from an apprenticeship of twenty-meter leads on small crags and end up having to bivouac.

When we reached the base of the wall, there were four other parties already on the climb, and they were yelling out belay signals and dropping stones on each other. Annalee and I tied in together and shortened the rope to about fifteen meters. I picked a line off to the left of the others to avoid the rockfall, and we started up. Annalee had never done any leading, and though we climbed together, I went first, picking the route and making certain that I was never directly above her so that I could see how she was doing. I kept flipping the rope behind blocks, and once in a while I'd leave a runner over a horn. Whenever I felt that there was a section that might give her any trouble, I'd brace myself and give her a belay. By moving together we quickly outdistanced the others and were soon dropping rocks on them!

Five hours after leaving the hut we were on the summit, having a cozy lunch in the warm sun. Down below on the slabs we could just make out the tiny dots of the others as they methodically belayed every inch of the way up. It was obvious they were in for a cold night.

Chuckling to ourselves, we took off down a gully on the west side, made a rappel, made another, and another, and. . . . Good God, had we screwed up! I hadn't bothered to check out the descent route! I had already left in all my slings and had used up my swami belt for rappel anchors. Now I began cutting up the nylon drawstrings on my pack. Next to go were my bootlaces. Then part of the rope. Well, we just made it back to the hut before nightfall. We weren't as smug as we'd been on top, but it was certainly warmer for us than it was for the others.

Tom Frost Photo

6

Security and the Rope

Ropes

Ropes are used for security on snow when the ice axe self-belay is not adequate and on ice whenever hand anchors cannot be completely trusted. One does not rope up merely because the consequences of a fall would be serious. The deciding factor is whether there is a *possibility* of falling. Strong words, yes, but not fanatical. I want to balance out the factors of complete security and being able to move fast. Of course, the guide with a client or a leader with a weak partner must accept completely the responsibility for their safety. This usually means that they must be roped at all times, although the belay need only be potential if the leader has the situation well in hand.

A 9- or 11-millimeter by 46-meter kernmantel rope is usually standard for ice climbing, although for big alpine climbs some hotshots use ropes up to 90 meters long to increase their speed. A 7- or 8-millimeter rope may be carried to use for rappelling and occasional light hauling. The cordage should be rounded off with 5 or 10 meters of 10-millimeter-wide webbing or similar material to allow for anchoring rappels.

There are many methods of roping up, ranging from simply running the climbing rope around the waist with a bowline to the truss-like harness systems. It's up to the individual to choose between simplicity/convenience and complexity/extreme safety. Simplicity is often safer in the end because it is less confusing, more versatile, doesn't give a false sense of security, and encourages all-important speed. A simple system is to wrap 5 meters or so of 20- or 30-millimeter webbing around the waist (the *swami belt*) and tie it with a ring bend. The rope is then tied through all the loops with a one-and-a-half fisherman's knot or with a figure-eight knot run back through itself. If dangerous glacier travel is anticipated, you may want to add *leg loops* to your swami. Just use two of your regular single- or double-length climbing runners and rig them as leg loops or a seat. Tie everything in together with the climbing rope, not carabiners! The fewer links in the safety chain, the better.

Anchors

Although the ice axe can serve as a superb anchor in some kinds of snow, there are times when the snow is either too hard or too soft for the *ice axe anchor* to be effective. Other anchors must be found. Three distinct methods are in use today: *screws* or *pickets*, *deadmen*, and *bollards*.

In fairly hard snow you can drive in long *ice screws* or *snow pickets* and belay anchored to these. Snow pickets are made of angle or T-shaped aluminum with holes drilled near the top end for a loop of webbing. The length need only be 50 centimeters for hard-snow conditions, but they must be up to a meter long for use in soft snow.

The *deadman* is usually the best anchor for very soft snow. Several variations exist on the basic theme of a rectangular aluminum plate which is buried in the snow by pounding it in at an approximately 45-degree angle to the direction of the load. A steel cable, with a loop in the end to clip into, runs perpendicular from the plate toward the direction of the belayer. By setting a deadman in the snow and arranging the suspension to pull slightly harder on the inner end, this device has been made to "fly" deeper into the snow the harder it is loaded. This sounds like it provides absolute security in very soft snow, but there *are* some problems. If a deadman isn't set at just the right angle, it can pull out. It has been known to dig deeper into the snow until it hits ice or an old hard crust. When this happens, the deadman can glance off and pull out.

In soft snow the deadman should be buried as deeply as possible. In hard snow it is necessary to hammer the plate in or to cut a suitably shaped slot. Remember that the angle between the plate and the direction of pull must be as near to 45 degrees as possible. The snow in front of the plate must not be disturbed except for a slot which must be cut for the cable. This slot must be cut in all types of snow and kept as narrow as possible. Viewed from above, the wire must be at right angles to the plate. If possible, test-load the anchor to ensure that it beds in correctly.

Another deadman-type anchor for soft snow is the ice axe: bury it horizontally across the slope as deeply as possible and tie in to the middle of the shaft with a prusik knot. A pack stuffed into a hole and then buried can also make a good anchor.

Of all the anchors for snow and ice, I have found the *bollard* to be the most valuable. Except for use as a rappel anchor, this con-structed "horn" has been overlooked by ice climbers probably because it is just too simple (it's much the same as the rockclimber who automatically bangs in a piton instead of placing a sling over a perfectly good horn of rock).

John Cunningham descending from an ice bollard on Ben Nevis.

The strength of a bollard is proportional to its size and to the hardness of the snow or ice. Even in soft snow a properly con-structed bollard can hold hundreds of kilograms, and on ice it can be so strong that the rope is the weak link. With experience it can be set up in the same amount of time that it takes to place a deadman or put in a piton anchor. I once climbed for a month with John Cunningham on Ben Nevis, where we did many of the classic ice climbs; in that time we constructed more bollards than we placed ice or rock pegs. We also never used a deadman, yet we did many of the climbs in very good time.

A bollard on ice needs to be only thirty centimeters in diameter, but on soft snow it may have to be two meters across and half a meter deep. If the snow is compactable, you should stamp it down before you cut a groove for the rope. Don't leave any slack in the anchor rope and make sure you shape the slot like the head of a mushroom so that the rope cannot jump out.

Snow and Ice Belays

You find yourself properly tied in and possessed of a knowledge of how to safely anchor yourself. But now you wonder how to safeguard your partner on this strange, slippery surface.

You already know the *simple hip belay* from rockclimbing that works so well when you're up to your armpits in a slot on an alpine ridge, straddling a tree on a Yosemite wall, sitting in a scoop on a granite dome, or dangling your feet off the edge of a back-sloping quartzite ledge. On rock the best belay is a secure sitting position from which you can't be pulled off; the easiest and most secure snow belays are no different.

Sitting hip belay. Note how legs are straight and feet are braced. Even the axe is used as an extra brace.

The simplest snow belay is a *sitting hip belay*. You can be down in a shallow crevasse, sitting in a well-formed suncup, up to your elbows in a moat, behind a serac, or braced against a rock that has melted itself into the slope. You can dig a hole in soft snow and plop into it; this is the "bucket belay." In harder snow a moment's chopping can quickly improve a marginal seat. A secure seat against downward pulls will work for most leading: since snow climbing will rarely be protected between stances, a falling leader will end up below his belayer. These sitting hip belays are not the most common snow belays, but they are the easiest transition from rockclimbing.

Snow is more often uniformly smooth than rock and lacks the convenient natural belay stances. The most obvious belay possibility is to use the ice axe. Dozens of ice axe belays have been proposed; most of them are complicated, flimsy, dangerous, and absurd. Even the best can be dangerously weak in soft snow.

Rockclimbing experience would suggest the *anchored hip belay* as a logical solution. Stick the axe in uphill, tie yourself to it, and belay. It's simple and logical but dangerous as well. This belay is rarely strong because the tie-in to the axe is always on the surface, next to the weakest snow. Under a load the axe cuts through this soft snow, the pull on the axe becomes outward, and it comes popping out. The strongest and fastest belays are those with the body holding the axe in place. Of these the boot-axe and hip-axe belays are the most reliable.

The *boot-axe belay* is usually the most secure belay for moderate slopes. To set up, begin by ramming your axe's shaft straight down into the snow all the way to the head. Facing across the slope, stamp your uphill foot directly below the axe to brace it from shearing out. Run the rope around the shaft and arrange it so that it lies doubled over the boot. Manage the rope with your downhill hand while keeping your uphill hand on the head of the axe to prevent it from popping upward. Concentrate your body weight on the axe and on the foot bracing it. Brace your other foot downhill for balance and against downward pull, but keep your weight on your uphill foot next to the axe's shaft. This is the key to the belay. Don't forget to push down on the head of the axe with the uphill hand, but watch out that the rope doesn't run over one of your fingers. If the axe is only partly rammed in, the lower leg and knee can be effectively used to help brace the shaft.

During a fall the rope ends up going over the toe of the boot, around the shaft, back over the boot and around the ankle to be held by the downhill belay hand. The force of the fall will pull the boot and axe toward each other for material support. The rope is not wound around the ankle until after the initial jerk of the fall, when more friction is needed to slowly bring the person to a stop.

For obvious reasons the boot-axe belay becomes difficult to set up on steep slopes. For this situation it will be necessary to do a *hip-axe belay*. In fact, in some conditions with soft snow, I have found it to be more secure than the boot-axe belay. As with all ice

The boot-axe belay.

Security and the Rope

Hip-axe belay.

axe belays, the usual point of failure is the ice axe pulling out; thus it's important that the axe be well braced against both outward and upward pull. Jam the axe in as deeply as possible with the wide side of the shaft facing downhill to help prevent the axe from shearing through soft snow. Keep your downhill leg straight and firmly braced against a downward pull. Bend and brace your uphill leg, and buttress your hip and upper thigh against the head or shaft of the axe. Put downward force on the head with your uphill hand. This is extremely important in keeping the axe from popping out. Hold the rope in your downhill hand and string it around the hips and around the shaft of the axe as in a normal belay.

In a good hip-axe belay only part of the load is held by the implanted axe. Since the rest is held by the braced legs, it is really important to stomp out a good place to brace against. If any one of the three anchoring factors (the implanted axe, the braced leg, and the hand on the head) is not done properly, the belay will fail.

The *dynamic belay* theory of letting the rope run through a belayer's hands as more friction is gradually applied in an effort to hold a fall more gently has been standard American rockclimbing technique for thirty years. Lately, the new high-elongation perlon ropes, in combination with more reliable pitons, chocks, and slings, have made dynamic belaying on rock less necessary. However, snow climbing can have some of the most weakly anchored belays in mountaineering, and the dynamic belay is absolutely essential to the success of both the boot-axe and hip-axe belays. It is necessary not for easing the gut-strain on the leader but rather for reducing the peak load on the belayer and his anchor. It's that initial jerk that the concern is all about. If one can survive that, then it's not difficult to let the rope run, nor is it hard to stop it smoothly and gradually. A wet rope adds a lot of friction, and that has to be taken into account. Using 9-millimeter ropes will add more elasticity to the system. The important thing is to practice snow belays before they are needed, to find out their limitations in poor conditions, and to improve the dynamic ropehandling that will stretch their limitations. You must practice this belay until you automatically let the rope slide during that initial jerk. Fortunately, this is much easier than practicing rock belays; all you need is a snowslope with a good runout and a daredevil, slippery leader.

So far I have mentioned only belays where the ice axe can be rammed either all the way in or at least part way in. What about very hard snow or ice? When we think of belaying on ice, our modern minds automatically blank out all but ice-piton belays.

What if you are in the middle of an ice climb and you drop the hardware rack? Or perhaps to save weight you haven't brought enough ice pegs to do the job? Don't rule out the bollard, for it can enable you to do roped ascents of all of the classic snow and ice faces in the Alps just as safely as with pitons. In addition, you can save money, weight, and have the satisfaction of using "natural" protection.

Another ace in the hole can be the *ice axe pick anchor*. With curved picks and strong metal, fiberglass, and laminated wood shafts, the pick belay has become strong and secure. The pick of the ice axe, Alpine hammer, or North Wall hammer is driven into the ice as deeply as possible. Hammer it deeper with your other tool if need be, and clip either into the hole in the head or, preferably, into the wrist strap if it is strong. With the proper tools this belay will also hold a ton. John Cunningham likes to use a combination *bollard/pick anchor* that seems to be bombproof. Cut a bollard and place the axe over to the side. The anchor rope is looped over the bollard, threaded through the waist tie, and then half-hitched, leaving another loop which is then clipped into the ice axe. The load is equally distributed between both anchors. To prevent an upward pull on the belayer, the axe can be placed below the bollard, the rope being anchored in opposition from it to the bollard.

Pitoncraft

If the temperature is below freezing, almost any ice piton will work, for the piton melts the ice as it's being driven and seconds later the ice freezes it in place. Freezing temperatures are not all that common in summer, so I recommend using only the tube screw and the "Wart Hog" type of piton, since they both seem to work well in the critical conditions above freezing.

The *tube screw* has the greatest holding power of any ice piton; whenever possible use it in preference to all other types. To place a tube screw, make a hole with the axe or hammer pick, then hammer the screw in until the threads catch. Using another piton or the pick of a tool for leverage, screw the piton in. If the cutting teeth are kept sharp, it is often possible to seat the screw by hand. It is possible to insert even a 28-centimeter screw in just a few seconds by using the axe like a bit and brace.

The *Wart Hog* is not screwed but just hammered straight in with many light blows; the more brittle the ice, the lighter the blows. As you hammer the Wart Hog into hard ice, it will rotate a bit in a clockwise direction. The harder the ice, the more rotation. You

Removing the ice screw by rotating the axe like a brace and bit. Doug Ross Photo.

Security and the Rope

should anticipate this rotation by cocking the piton eye counter-clockwise before driving so that it rests downward when the piton is all the way in. In hard cold ice this may mean a full quarter turn.

The holding power of all ice pitons is more dependent on the angle of the pull and the stiffness of the piton than it is on the holding power of the threads or "warts." Whether an ice or rock piton is used, the normal right-angle load must become an outward load before the piton can come out. The piton must bend or shear through the ice until the load is outward. (For instance, you can't pull a nail with a claw hammer unless the nail bends.) All ice pitons, therefore, should be driven into the ice at an approximate angle of 45 to 60 degrees to the slope.

A Wart Hog should always be placed all the way into the ice. Never clip into one that is only part way in, and never tie one off, as it may break. Ice often has a soft, brittle top layer eight or ten centimeters thick. A Wart Hog fully driven into this type of ice is only a little stronger than one driven halfway in, because under a load the surface ice will crack away or the piton will shear or melt through the soft ice. Always clear away all the brittle or soft surface ice before placing any ice piton.

Tests indicate that certain tube screws will hold from 500 to 2,000 kilograms, depending on the hardness or brittleness of the snow or ice, the temperature, the angle of pull, and the length of the tube. The Wart Hog holds a maximum of 1,000 kilograms before it either breaks or pulls out.

The *boot/piton belay* is used on gentle slopes or on flat ground. An ice piton is placed, and the rope is clipped into a carabiner. The cramponed boot is placed on top of the piton with the inside point of the fourth pair (counting from the front) of crampon points going through the carabiner. By adjusting the distance between this point and the rope through the carabiner, you can vary greatly the amount of friction on the rope. The rope then goes over the instep of the boot and around the ankle. The belay hand controls the drag by the amount of wrap around the ankle just like a *boot/axe* belay.

On steep ice it is best to anchor the belayer directly to the piton and give a normal hip belay. With modern tube screws in solid ice, one piton is usually adequate for an anchor. If you wish, you can double up the anchor by placing a hammer or axe off to the side and anchoring to this.

I prefer to place my piton anchors as high as is comfortable—rather than at waist level—so that in holding a leader fall through

Ice piton being screwed in at the proper angle. And the boot-piton belay.

a protection piton, the force pulls the belayer upward, thus adding some dynamics to the system. To make sure you don't drop the belay rope, clip it into a carabiner around the waist tie.

Cramponing up an extremely steep slope of hard, smooth blue ice on a great alpine wall is not only physically tiring but may be one of the more mentally fatiguing aspects of alpine climbing. Certainly the most dangerous part is at the end of the lead, where you are strung out mentally, your legs are cramped, and you have to stand on tiny points and set up a belay. On this type of climbing the leader frequently prefers to forego putting in much protection and just "goes for it." Saving energy is climbing safer.

If you stretch out long leads in this manner, the belay had better be bombproof. Near the end of his pitch the leader looks for a protruding rock or a scoop where there is a lessening of the angle. Stop here, drive in the pick of your hand tool high above and hang on to it; this is your temporary belay. Make sure the pick is in securely and that the leash is tied to the waist or to a tight shoulder loop. With the ice axe cut a long enough step to splay both feet out horizontally. Now you can rest and put in the belay pitons. Even though in ideal conditions tube screws can hold over 2,000 kilograms, don't count on this; some ice, especially brittle ice, is unreliable. Unless time is an important factor, you should put in two pitons for a belay. One goes in about head high; tie into it with a clove hitch. Climb higher and put in another piton one or two meters above. Tie into this one also and put in an extra carabiner. Clip the belay rope into this upper piton and go back down to belay from the foothold. The second person is belayed directly through the extra carabiner of the top peg. When he comes up, exchanges hardware, and leads off, his first piece of protection is already in. Nothing is scarier than having twenty-four sharp points hanging over your head, so the leader stays off to the side and stretches out his next lead as far as his nerves or yours will allow. It is far better to hold a fifty- or seventy-five-meter fall through a piton than to take the full force with only a hip belay. Mechanical belay devices work out very well for this style of climbing.

Placing protection and setting up belays on vertical or overhanging ice takes a great deal of strength, skill, proper equipment, and forethought. The alternative, however, is protectionless climbing or a cop-out to artificial climbing. The problem is that you need two hands to place an ice piton and yet you can't let go of your tools without falling over backwards. The simplest method that I've worked out is this: drive in both hand tools solidly, particularly the axe which is held in the left hand (assuming you are right-

The series of photos on the following pages show Doug Robinson and the author on the first ascent of the central Leevining Icefall in the Sierra Nevada, 1970. Russ McLean Photos.

125

Security and the Rope

Placing an ice screw with the arm hanging from a wrist loop. Del Johns Photo. And stopping on a vertical section by hanging from a cow's tail and cliff hanger. Rob Taylor Photo.

handed). Take your hand out of the leash's loop, undo the twist, slip your whole arm through again right up to the elbow, and hang all your weight off this axe. Now your left hand is free to hold an ice piton while it is being driven in with the hammer. Another method utilizes a "cow's tail." This is a short cord tied permanently onto the waist tie with a cliffhanger, fifi hook, or carabiner on the end. After this is clipped into the wrist loop of the solidly implanted axe, you can sit back and relax while both hands are free to place a good tube screw. If you are using a Terrordactyl, you can hang the cliffhanger directly onto the top of the pick next to the ice to eliminate leverage. On very brittle ice you may want to lead with two hammers so that one can be used to drive in the other for a solid anchor. The second man can follow with both axes.

Potential Belays

You have succeeded in moving quite safely belayed, something of an accomplishment on a changeable surface like snow. But progress has been slow if you've had to stop and belay every pitch. So slow, in fact, that you don't have a chance of getting up the big alpine snow faces without inviting disaster from an afternoon avalanche, a thunderstorm, and/or soft snowbridges. You cannot make haste by setting up belays and moving one at a time.

Competent climbers will rarely require belaying on steep snow-slopes; instead they will rely on confidence, experience, and the self-belay. But everyone must be a beginner sometime, and all of us make mistakes. To be able to move safely and quickly on steep snow with a novice or a tired client is probably the most challenging act of guiding. The mountain guide has a responsibility to get his client up and down the mountain safely—and to protect his own skin at the same time. He knows they must move fast to get up safely, but he also knows that there is a chance the client will slip and pull both of them down the face. Many guides refuse to expose themselves to this danger and will not guide long, steep snow- and ice-climbs. Yet some old, experienced mountain guides are able to move together roped with their clients up the classic snow faces in relative safety. A sixth sense tells them when a client is liable to slip, where to keep the rope tight, when to glance back; this all requires technique, particularly the ability to set up a *potential belay*. No person should call himself a mountain guide until he acquires this ability to set up some sort of instant belay on various-angled snowslopes while "on the fly."

Whenever any party is roped together, all the ropemates should be prepared to check a fall at a moment's notice. There are various methods for doing this, depending on the situation. You need a belay that is mostly potential, yet it must be applied quickly, almost instantly, in an emergency. A strong party will usually do the big snow faces roped up but moving together. The rope is kept on to be used for the occasional belay on steep bulges or patches of ice. When climbing simultaneously (whether on rock, snow, or for glacier travel), the rope must be shortened. Each person takes up some small coils, just large enough to go over the shoulder and hang down to just above the waist. The climber then ties in with a bowline-on-a-coil through the swami or harness and around the coil.

One system for climbing together on very steep snowslopes utilizes a cord from the waist to the ice axe. I use my normal prusik sling described in the crevasse rescue section. I tie one end into my waist tie and loop the other end over the shaft of the axe, the loop being held by my hand on the head of the axe. In the *piolet manche* position, going straight uphill, I am self-belayed as well as somewhat belaying my ropemates. Should I see a rock or a small avalanche coming, I thrust in the axe and drop the loop so that it rests on the snow to prevent leverage.

The boot-axe belay adapts well to moving together on moderate and steep slopes. The rope going to the leader is held by the axe hand and is kept around the uphill side of the shaft. A few coils of rope are held by the other hand. To do a quick boot-belay, pounce on your ice axe, thrusting it in right next to your uphill foot. At the same time drop the belay rope so it slides down the shaft to eliminate leverage. Brace your downhill foot while dropping the coils you have been carrying, re-grasp the rope and give a dynamic belay. All the weight is concentrated on the uphill foot bracing the axe and on the uphill hand holding the axe in place. Except for the surprise, the belay is carried out exactly like a prearranged one. This is a very effective belay if it has been practiced to the point where it is instinctive. It is complicated and difficult to do all these motions at once, but it can be made even more complicated. For instance, you can drive your axe in anywhere and *then* pick up your uphill foot and brace against it, thus adding one extra step and losing a few precious seconds. Once again, practice is the key.

One of the most important factors in the success of any *potential* or *instant belay* is the friction of the rope dragging on the surface of the snow. For example, it is much easier to hold a leader fall if the leader is way off to the side and above, rather than directly above the belayer. The friction of the rope on the snow will absorb a good deal of the force of the fall. A good guide will always use

The standard method for shortening the rope. Finish by tying a bowline on a coil. Tom Frost Photo.

this factor to his advantage. Besides, he can always keep the client in his peripheral vision if he is off slightly to the side.

Roped Descents

Descent on extremely steep snow or ice is done by rappel. Ice pitons or snow pickets can be left as the rappel anchor. One of the best and certainly least expensive rappel points is a snow or ice *bollard* cut into the slope. If the snow is soft, do not put the rope directly around the bollard; instead use a separate sling to facilitate pulling down the rappel rope. You can also reinforce the bollard by stamping the snow down and lining the uphill side with rocks or sticks to distribute the load.

Every rappel can be self-belayed, and it is amazing that this is not practiced more often, for it is very simple. It is especially important where there is danger of falling rock or ice. Simply tie a prusik knot around the rappel rope and clip it to the waist loop. A three-wrap prusik with 5- or 6-millimeter cord will provide greater security than the usual two wraps on nylon ropes, especially if they are wet or icy. Keep the knot loose on the rope and cupped in the uphill hand as it slides along. If you lose control of the rappel the knot tightens. But make sure the prusik loop is not so long that the knot can tighten up out of your reach!

Opposite, climbing together on the Window Route, Mount Kenya. Tom Frost Photo.

Security and the Rope

In the moat of the Palisade Glacier,
Sierra Nevada. Tom Frost Photo.

We were walking over the avalanche debris of the Great Gully on our way to Crowberry when an ominous croak split the silence. Two black ravens swooped over the Buachaille. John Cunningham's words echoed in my head: "Raven's the hardest climb in the Coe, and you should do it if it's in good nick."

We soloed up the perfect styrofoam all the way to the first giant chockstone, which we mounted with a mere couple of grunts. More perfect snow. When the next block offered resistance, it was promptly overkilled with "cunning rope maneuvers." Authorization was Ian Clough's *Guide*: "Speed is the critical factor . . . there is no need for an artificial code of rules. . . ." Right on.

Up next was another barricade, with a dank belay cave. Leaning over the roof was a pillar ladder of meringue which collapsed with the tail man. We were already one pitch above it when we spotted Hamish's Barefoot Exit going to the left. Going back meant having to lose out to that last motha chock. Anyhow, it was pretty secure being in the slit, and higher up it looked even darker and quieter.

Escape was now defined in a fading shaft of light coming over a great stone stuck between two icy walls. The verglas was too thick for vibram and too thin for crampons, while the distance between the wall was a bridge—or more. The game was to maximize your body and scratch up as high as you could before your legs gave. At least there was a nice soft snow bottom to the chimney. Spread-eagling with his crampons, Doug Tompkins managed three meters before he jumped. Trying a Nureyev split, I did four and lost it. Doug got to six and . . . at ten meters the tip of a knifeblade held for a tie-off just before my legs accordioned. The thin ray of light was growing faint as I was winched up to the peg for one last effort. Taking a wee rest in a sling, I swore that next time I came back to the Scottish winter I'd be better fit for climbing rock! The next ten meters to the stone was indeed a shaky endeavor.

All that was left now was the slot that Hamish had slept under on his solo. Tompkins attacked the thin ice and powder snow with tied-off screws and delicate body English. After what seemed an hour, a long AHOOYA! We weren't on top, but we were OUT!

7
Keeping Your Head about You

The Changing Mountain

The earth, cooling and wrinkling, pushes up mountains. Gravity calls them down. These improbable minarets stand up in a sea of air that is itself changing—cycling in the water that the sun stole from the sea and flinging it back to earth. When the ocean of air runs into rock wrinkles standing up into the sky, it gets turned off course and is raised and cooled. Inevitably it fights back, pouring torrents of wind and water—much of it crystallized—onto the rocky heights. All that water soon begins its journey downhill, and inevitably it will take some rock with it. Rockfall, waterfall, icefall, avalanche: the climber must deal with each in turn or become their victim. Knowledge is power is life.

Nowhere on the planet are the forces of change more active and evident than in the mountains. Mountain building is often abrupt, and ever after their destruction is ceaseless. The climber thrusts himself into the midst of this metamorphosis. Rockclimbers think their world stable, their creations everlasting as they climb the surface of the outermost exfoliation shell while it is busy delaminating from the mountain. Alpinists are less illusioned; frost-wedging

Opposite, on the north face of Cima di Rosso, in the Bergell Alps. John Cleare Photo.

and thermal cracking have left their landscape more shattered, loose at hand, and hanging overhead. They have learned to tiptoe.

Change may be relentless, but it is not often random. As Einstein said, "God does not play dice with the Universe." The spindrift avalanches of new snow fluffing off a steep face fall into a clockwork pattern. The slides in a gully are coming three minutes apart; there goes another—now quickly scuttle across. Most mountain hazards are not that precise, yet they do follow some pattern of daily or seasonal cycles. The mountaineer's best defense is timing. Climb snowfields when they are frozen into a good working surface, glissade just as the surface has thawed, and be gone by the time softness has reached deep enough for the slope to avalanche. Travel light and move fast; speed is safety.

On a rock crag it is possible to have nearly complete control over the climbing situation. The loose handholds have been culled by generations of climbers; guidebooks and detailed drawings describe all the difficulties to be encountered; and the climber need concern himself only with choosing a climb within his capabilities. Snow and ice is a different story. The medium is a plastic material, the most variable of all plastic media. And it is found not on city crags but in the highest ranges, where it is influenced by the fickle and uncontrollable weather.

The north face of the Aiguille de Triolet. Jurgen Winkler Photo.

It isn't long before the novice ice climber learns the techniques necessary to do some of the great ice climbs, but to do them safely

Page 137, *The fourth pitch of Repentance, Canon Mountain, New Hampshire. Henry Barber Photo.*

Page 138, *Starting off from the Col of Hope on the Cerro Torre, Patagonia. John Bragg Photo.*

Page 139, *The author on the ice ribbon, Mount Kenya. Tom Frost Photo.*

Page 140, *Mixed climbing in New England. Dale Bard Photo.*

Page 141, *The 275-meter high Vettisfossen Falls, Norway. Henry Barber Photo.*

Page 142, *John Cunningham on the Bosson Glacier, Chamonix, France.*

Page 143, *Fred Wright on the southeast ridge of Mount McKinley, Alaska. Peter Lev Photo.*

Page 144, *The author and John Cunningham near the top of Ben Nevis. Paul Braithwaite Photo.*

takes years of trial-and-error experience. The actual climbing on snow and ice may be fairly straightforward, but judging the conditions is a deep and complicated art. To attempt to describe in this book all the nuances of the art would not only be folly but would also rob the aspiring ice climber of one of the great values of the mountain experience—the joy of discovery. A few suggestions on the more frequent dangers are in order, however, so that the novice will at least have a chance to survive his first big alpine adventure.

Corniced Ridges

The cornice, a real danger to contend with on a snowy ridge, is the overhanging brow of snow that caps the leeward side of a ridge, cantilevering out from its moorings as wind piles on more snow until it falls of its own weight—or gets knocked off. Cornices in the Alps are the largest in the late winter and spring. In the Andes and Himalaya they are dangerous year round. Cornices can be seen easily when approached from the leeward side but are less obvious from the windward. Any sharp ridge that appears flattened must be considered suspicious. Give all cornices a wide berth! The line of break normally follows the angle of the slope overhung by the cornice and not a vertical line. Double cornices are seen occasionally.

Couloirs

Those deep, dark slots in a mountain known as couloirs are often the most obvious routes of ascent. They are usually lower angled than the enclosing cliffs and appear to have easier climbing. This would be fine if they were not also the route of preference for falling rock and ice, or avalanches of snow. Not only are they natural funnels but their very existence indicates weak, fractured rock. Examine the slope at the base of the couloir for evidence of fresh rockfall, but do not be misled if the snow is clean. The bergschrund can collect falling rock, or the debris may be hidden in soft snow. Stonefall is at its worst in the morning, just after the sun hits the faces and melts the ice bond holding the rocks together. It can also be bad for a brief period in the afternoon when freezing water in cracks expands and pushes off the stones.

The sun strikes the mountain top first thing in the morning. On a north-facing couloir it may shine up high for only a brief time. Plan your climb so you are not in an exposed place when this happens. Stonefall in the Canadian Rockies (with its ledges piled up at maximum angle with scree and gravel) is particularly bad

A cornice on the northwest ridge of Illimani, Cordillera Real, Bolivia. This cornice could break far inside the line of steps. Herbert Ziegenhardt Photo.

145

during a heavy rainfall. Plan the belay stances so that they are protected from above. If there is a potential danger from other parties dislodging rocks or ice, be the first on the climb. It is a far greater safety factor in being the top rope on the climb than it is to wear a crash helmet.

Since snow couloirs often have cornices (especially in winter or spring), make sure you can see the top before you start up. Cornices are not only a danger in themselves; they can create rockfall or set off unstable snowslopes.

The center of the couloir is the most dangerous section. If the gully winds around, use your head and decide which side is safer to be on and use the *moat*, the crevasse-like gap at the edge of the gully where the ice has melted away from the rock. Not only does the moat promise sheltered belay stances, but it often offers some interesting Scottish-style climbing with one foot on rock, one on ice. On the Eiger's north wall experienced alpinists climb the famous Second Icefield up its relatively safe right side, then traverse the top moat to the left, since the steep cliff above offers protection from rockfall. The foolish climber will hack his way diagonally across the slope and be fully exposed to rockfall for twenty rope lengths. So, remember: moats offer natural belay stances, protection from rockfall, and often easier climbing.

Conditions in couloirs change during the season, and a couloir that is normally a death trap in July can be a safe, enjoyable climb in September. The great ice gullies in the Sierra Nevada have no rockfall in the autumn climbing season.

The strong sun and bitterly cold nights of the mountains of the equator produce huge, ten-meter-long icicles that perch vulture-like on the lips of overhangs. These icicles seem to break off most often just before light; they must be most brittle during the coldest part of the night.

Snowslopes

If timing is important in climbing gullies because of stonefall, it is important on snowslopes because the condition of the snow can change so dramatically. Dawn's crunchy crust can turn to mid-morning wallow, and this may be followed shortly by the daily avalanche. I remember that we started out from the Argentière hut at one A.M. to climb the north face of the Aiguille Verte. We were on the summit just after dawn and down the Whymper Couloir before it had a chance to avalanche from the hot sun. After ten A.M. the Whymper is often too dangerous to descend; the alternate is a long, arduous mixed descent of the Grand Rocheuse

In the Diamond Couloir, Mount Kenya. Tom Frost Photo.

Buttress. Alpine starts are not only necessary to find the snow in good frozen condition but are often essential to the descents. They also avoid the afternoon thunder and lightning storms typical of high mountains. The best time to forecast the day's weather is around three A.M., the hour when the old guides are always out on the hut terrace checking the temperature, the brightness of the stars, and the wind. A cloudy sky can hold ground heat like a blanket, making it more likely that the snow is not freezing. "Clear and cold" has become the alpine byline for good weather.

Most of the big alpine snow climbs are done in June or July, when the faces are composed of frozen firn snow. This has just the right crunchiness for full crampon penetration and lightning fast French technique. By August the slopes show much bare ice, and the climbs are considered "out of condition." This no longer needs to be the case with the new equipment and techniques. It is often better to do the climbs in ice conditions. The climbing is far more exciting, the protection bombproof, and there is no danger of avalanches. September and October are often the best months for snow and ice or mixed climbing in the Alps. I've seen perfect weather in Chamonix for the whole month of October and half of November—cold, clear days with brickhard snow, no rockfall, no tourists; only the deep solitude of the giant peaks frozen in the autumn silence.

Glaciers

In the Alps many climbers and porters with heavy loads go unroped on snow-covered glaciers. The novice climber is tempted to do the same. Although there may be a well-worn path, the fact remains that these people are walking over potentially dangerous holes. You have only to come back later to see all the yawning gaps that were smooth snowslopes a week before to realize the foolishness of being unroped on a snow-covered glacier. Seasoned glacier climbers can get away with a lot because of their experience and sixth sense in picking the right path and smelling out hidden crevasses. The novice climber, however, must allow more leeway for errors in judgment, since there's a blue eternity down there if he guesses wrong. A bare glacier without concealing snow is much easier to deal with.

The middle of a glacier generally has the fewest crevasses. On a bend, the outside edge will be more badly crevassed than the inner edge. The roped party should maintain a path at right angles to the general trend of the crevasses. But don't forget that it's possible for the entire party to be walking directly over a wide crevasse.

147

Probing for hidden crevasses with the ice axe (again a case against very short axes) is of value according to the climber's experience: that is, his sensitivity to changes in resistance and his ability to interpret the meaning of those changes.

It is essential that all the members of a rope team not fall into the same crevasse, yet it is common for a party to cluster close together during rest stops. Group together only when it is certain that no crevasse exists. I like to stop for lunch right on the edge of an open crevasse where I can see exactly the obvious danger.

Skis distribute the weight more evenly over snowbridges and their use allows you to travel in relative safety on otherwise dangerous glaciers. I will discuss skis more in a later chapter.

A snowbridge that is frozen hard and safe in the morning can become impassable by afternoon. Time your climbs accordingly

The Yentna Glacier and Great Icefall descending from the Russell Plateau, Alaska. Bradford Washburn Photo.

and don't get into one-way traps. You may want to crawl over the weaker bridges to spread out your weight more evenly. Before jumping over crevasses, consider that the edges may be overhangs of corniced snow waiting for your impact to collapse them. Going into a roll on the other side can sometimes help, or you can land with your axe in *piolet ancre* position.

The stability of seracs (giant blocks of snow usually found in ice-falls) is determined mostly by the movement of the glacier and is less affected by warmth or weather. Remember that they can come down any time during the day or night. These falling walls of ice are the biggest killers in Himalayan climbing. Some climbers go to these mountains with an Alpine scale of reality. They often do not realize that the little hanging serac a mile above their heads is actually a huge, overhanging cliff. Not only is this perched ice capable of snuffing out an entire base camp, but it can also set off an avalanche-prone slope that may travel for miles, even going up the opposite side of the valley for a thousand feet.

Crevasse Rescue

As implied earlier, "dry" glaciers, free of their cover of snow, have their crevasses totally visible, and it is not necessary to use the rope. In the following discussion of crevasse rescue I will be referring to snow-covered glaciers.

Just as every rockclimber will eventually take a fall, so is it that sooner or later almost everyone who does any alpine climbing falls into a crevasse. The most dangerous ones are the hidden ones, innocently masquerading as solid surfaces.

There are five basic safety rules for glacier travel: (1) Always use the rope. (2) The belayer must be able to anchor the rope after the fall. (3) The fallen climber must be prepared to get himself out. (4) The belayer must be able to send down either the end of the rope or another rope to the fallen climber. (5) The belayer must know how to extricate an unconscious victim. On a typical day of glacier travel, the climber might end up using all these "rules." They will be described in detail below.

The method of roping up on a glacier is the same as the one I have already recommended for snow climbing. Tie the end of the rope to the swami belt or harness. Each person then takes up some small coils, perhaps a third of the rope per man if there are two climbers. The coils should be barely large enough to go over the shoulder and hang diagonally down to the waist. A bowline-on-a-coil is tied around the swami and the coil. You should have at least ten meters of rope between each person (don't forget that crevasses ten meters wide or more are not uncommon!). A rope of three is safer than a rope of two; in fact, having more than one person on the surface is all but essential for removing an unconscious victim. If there are three climbers, rope up with two ropes to ensure that plenty of spare rope remains on the surface to help the one who has foundered.

Each person should carry either two or three prusik slings. These are made from about two-and-a-half meters of five-millimeter nylon. Using prusik knots, attach the slings to the rope just in front of your waist tie. The other ends, each with a foot loop, are carried

On a glacier in the Cordillera Vilcabamba, Peru. George Bell Photo.

Keeping Your Head about You

A shortened rope, with a bowline on a coil and prusiks in place.

in the pockets to keep them out of the way. The prusik loops can also be kept very small, and, when the need arises, étriers can be attached to them. The optional third prusik is for the chest. It can make an overhanging prusik much more comfortable. This sling can either stay in the pocket or, on heavily crevassed areas and with a monster pack, be placed on the rope above the leg prusiks and looped around the chest. If you choose not to use a chest prusik, then be sure to tuck the upper leg sling inside of the waist tie; this will help keep you from flipping over backwards when in mid-air. The pack is worn over everything, and if it is heavy it should have an attached cord, the end of which is clipped into the waist tie. This allows one to dangle the pack when necessary.

"Keep a dry rope" is a good rule for walking roped on a glacier. This means keeping the slack to a minimum. A well-held fall on a reasonably tight rope will require only a mantleshelf to get out of a crevasse. Hand coils amount to slack between climbers and slack obviously increases the length of the fall. The second man should carry only two or three small coils—just enough to keep the party moving smoothly together and to give him time to brace for the leader's fall.

If someone suddenly disappears, the first action falls to the rope-mates left on the surface, who instantly become belayers. The obvious fear of being yanked off one's feet and sucked into the crevasse in the wake of a fallen partner is greatly exaggerated. It would be fairly easy for the belayer to lose control on a bare-ice glacier, but that is unlikely since all the slots are exposed and clearly visible. The chance of falling into a crevasse is obviously much greater when snow lies on the glacier, muffling its contours and concealing secret slots. Not being sure if he's walking on snow-covered ice or snow-covered air can keep things exciting for the leader, but it virtually assures the second of holding a fall as long as he has kept the rope reasonably tight. When the leader falls, the rope is pulled into the snow along the lip of the crevasse, deeply burying itself. The snow absorbs most of the shock. Keeping the leader on a tight rope is the key, but it's not as easy as it sounds, since glacier travel can involve a lot of routefinding and serpentine winding. Thin snowbridges or questionable jumps can be protected by a quick boot-axe belay.

Dangling in the crevasse, the leader is wishing he had been probing more energetically with his axe. Since his pack is either pulling him over backwards or has actually succeeded in turning him upside down, his first and correct instinct is to get rid of it. After checking to be sure the pack is clipped in, he slips out of it. This lowers his center of gravity so that he can at least be upright. Now he takes out the top prusik sling and "sits" in it, as if in an étrier. It is very difficult when carrying a heavy pack even to make a move while dangling on the end of a rope, so it may prove better first to sit in the prusik and then take off the pack. If the pack is very heavy, it may be necessary to tie it into the end of the rope to be pulled up later. Or it can be hauled up on an extra rope sent by the belayer.

The belayer has used his own prusik slings to anchor the rope to his ice axe, ice screw, bollard, or whatever. With his arms free he can take off his rope coil and throw it down to the fallen person, who may want to stop spinning by prusiking on both ropes. The fallen climber will certainly need that extra rope to get over the lip of the crevasse, since his climbing line is by now buried deeply in the soft snow. The second rope will be most effective if the

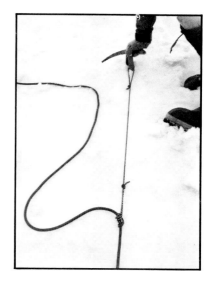

belayer pads the edge of the crevasse where the rope goes over; the use of a rucksack or ice axe handle will help keep the rope from sinking into the soft snow. Foot loops knotted in the rope can be useful in some situations. Meanwhile, the climber in the crevasse is continuing to prusik up both ropes, standing on one rope while moving the prusik higher on the other.

If a spare line or another end is not available, the fallen person prusiks up to the lip, where the rope is stuck in a deep groove. By this time he is probably trailing a bit of slack, so he ties in again to his climbing rope below his prusiks, unties his original waist tie, and sends up the free end of the rope.

Keeping Your Head about You

The situation thus far described assumes the worst possible landing: a mid-air dangle at the end of the rope. Obviously, this isn't always the case. Before blindly beginning the rope tricks of extrication, look around, then consider this mountaineering problem you've dropped in on. Is it a narrow slot? Chimneying with crampons is fairly easy. If the wall is less than vertical, you may be able to front-point out with tension from above. Perhaps there's a solid snowbridge or ice shelf below. It's easy to get yourself lowered; then you can size up the situation without that insistent tug on your ribs. Now, can you walk out the end? Traverse to a narrow section and chimney up? Find a side slot and back-door your way out? Jam an ice sliver? Ingenuity here can save a lot of effort and maybe avoid that sickening slow spin when prusiking up the rope.

Of course, these methods all depend on the fallen person being able to extricate himself. But if he is severely injured or unconscious, the matter of rescue becomes much more complicated and serious, especially for a rope of two. After tying off the rope, the belayer's first concern is to see that his friend is not being strangled by a swami belt tight on his ribs and stomach. He may have to go down and construct a seat sling, but a little preventive forethought is much easier. Before you start your glacier travel a runner can be twisted into quite an effective set of leg loops. Turn the runner into a "figure-eight" and put one leg in each loop. Then tie into the rope through both the leg loop and the swami. It's a good idea to tie in this way any time you're going onto a dangerous glacier. In a fall much of the stress will come onto these leg loops, and the strangulation problem is minimized. For a rope of two on a dangerous glacier it's a good idea to have all prusiks and leg loops in place and perhaps rope up with a double rope.

To pull an unconscious victim from a crevasse there are a number of common-sense methods which utilize the mechanical advantage of pulleys, prusiks, or jumars. The chief problem encountered is usually the amazing friction which develops between a wet rope and the ice or snow. Whatever fancy system is employed is doomed to failure unless the edge of the crevasse is well padded.

Once you are roped and capable of all possible rescues, you are prepared to delve safely into the finer arts of glacier travel: that is, to travel on them without visiting any of the slots along the way. You will learn to detect subtleties on the snow surface that speak of a slot beneath. You will learn the value of overview from a high point nearby, and you will learn to plan a line and hold to it. You will learn to predict the condition of a glacier from the map or from experiences in the next valley. By working on your rope-handling you will better be able to run the gauntlet of a crevasse field quickly and smoothly.

Speed and Safety

Though the "rules" and suggestions mentioned thus far in this chapter are very important for your overall safety, there is another factor which is equally important: speed. This might sound like a contradiction, for one thinks of those patient mountaineers constantly safeguarding every move as being the safest. In another sphere, speeding cars have always been thought of as synonymous with reckless driving. How is the speedy climber to avoid the same stigma?

Mountains are dangerous, and the faster and more dynamic you are under dangerous conditions, the safer you will be. The slower a rope goes, the more vulnerable it is to both systematic and random attacks from both the mountain and the volatile sky it penetrates. The best security against these alpine hazards, better than hard hats, radios, down bivouac gear, or the "ten essentials," is to be up and off the mountain when it erupts.

It is difficult for the British or American climber going to the Alps for the first time to understand the speed trip that all the hot continental climbers are on. But a few close calls in those big mountains will serve to prove the maxim: *speed is safety*.

To be able to move fast in the mountains, you must be physically fit and acclimatized, make correct routefinding decisions, use efficient rope management procedures, carry light packs, and resolve technical difficulties efficiently. Basically, it comes down to being experienced and fit and having a desire to push one's limits.

Moving fast and light in the mountains can also be extremely satisfying. If man obtains pleasure from running around an oval track, leaping over hurdles, or jogging through the woods, then perhaps the mountains, with all their varied terrain, uncontrived problems, and pure difficulties, are the ideal playground for attaining the pure physical joy of movement. Man was not meant to carry his home on his back or to travel at a snail's pace—he delights in being dynamic.

Below, I have listed a number of ways of increasing speed when moving over the snowy mountains. If only a few minutes can be saved from each of them, hours will be the final sum saved on a long day's climb.

Running risks is not the object of the game, but it's a part of it. Only a lengthy experience, enabling observations to be stored up both in memory and the subconscious, endows a few climbers with a sort of instinct not only for detecting danger, but for estimating its seriousness.

—Lionel Terray
Conquistadors of the
Useless

1. Push yourself: desire to move faster.

2. Get in good physical condition by training. Stay high (in the altitude sense of the word!) during periods of bad weather so as to remain acclimatized.

3. Learn about local weather conditions to avoid being pinned down by storms.

4. Memorize the ascent and descent routes so that you can leave the guidebook behind. Study a crevassed glacier from above and plot your route ahead of time.

5. Get an early start to avoid the party ahead of you, the afternoon avalanche, the inevitable thunderstorm, the soft snowbridge which must be bypassed, the swollen river, and the evening freeze that forces you to crampon down the slope which you could have glissaded an hour before.

6. Adopt a steady pace that you can maintain for hours without stopping or perspiring.

7. Let the strongest climber lead all the way through.

8. Eat and drink frequently to conserve energy. Rather than stopping and "brewing up," carry tea or soup in a vacuum bottle.

9. Carry light packs, and leave most of the "ten essentials" and other impedimenta behind. Remember: if you take bivouac equipment along, you will bivouac.

10. Arrange the pack so that the items you most likely will need in the course of a climb are easily available.

11. Use extra-long ropes to cut down the number of belay stances on ice.

12. Avoid using complicated harnesses which require a tedious untying to remove or put on clothing.

13. Use chocks and natural protection instead of rock pitons; use bollards instead of deadmen and ice pitons.

14. Use a 70-centimeter ice axe instead of a 55-centimeter one. This will give you an extra reach.

15. Think twice before putting on crampons for

that short little section. Cutting a few steps might be faster.

16. Learn to put your crampons on in two or three minutes. Carry them in a convenient place, and forget about the rubber tip protectors.

17. Keep your tools sharp.

18. Learn to crampon quickly across dangerous avalanche chutes and stonefall gullies. The fastest cramponing technique is akin to running on all fours. Hold two axes, or other tools, in *piolet panne* and crab across the slope.

19. If really pushed for time, follow an ice pitch on tension, using nothing for the hands. Or use the rope as a hand rail.

20. Don't drive in the axe for self-belay when following in steps. Depend instead on balance, and use the other steps for handholds.

21. Avoid cutting long ladders of steps.

22. Don't use *piolet traction* for your hands if you can get away with using just the axe. Try rock-climbing an ice pitch with just your crampons and your hands on the ice.

23. Solo snow climbs using the ice axe self-belay. Do the more difficult climbs roped up, but move together. Stop and belay only if absolutely necessary. Avoid ropes of three.

24. In the winter, know the snow conditions so that you always travel on the stable wind pack.

25. Down climb. Don't rappel unless absolutely necessary.

26. Face outward when descending whenever possible. Only when it gets really steep should you face sideways. As a last resort face inward.

27. Learn to be an excellent glissader. It takes only a few minutes to glissade a 500-meter slope, but it will take half an hour to heel down.

Ruedi Homberger Photo

I asked him for the rope, and he said, "You've got it." Well, I didn't, and we weren't about to go all the way back to the lodge to get it. So we decided to drop down into the corrie and solo some Grade III's on Hell's Lum. It was blowing a blizzard up on the plateau, but it wasn't snowing lower, and there were patches of blue sky. Frost feathers were growing on our wool clothes, and our eyelids and nose hairs were all frozen over; it was a typical day in Scotland's Cairngorms.

Doug Tompkins was ahead, cramponing and traversing across some hard wind pack. All of a sudden my rectum clutched up like a poodle's when it sees a bulldog, and I said to Doug, "Hey man, this snow feels really funny. Let's get. . . ." Pop! and we were off. A meter-thick slab broke off right at our feet, and we were both left hanging by our ice axes, which luckily we had planted high.

Later on that day we watched a student from John Cunningham's class drop his pack; it rolled down almost to the Shelter Stone. Johnny told him to go way over to the south side before going down to get it. But he didn't go far enough, and we watched him ride out a beauty! All these big blocks were rolling and grinding, but he stayed on top the whole way. A lucky kid!

The other close call I had in Scotland was on Ben Nevis. We were filming from near the base of Comb Buttress, and, though the spring thaw was on, the snow didn't seem overly dangerous. I had the rope on and was standing around when I caught a glimpse of Cunningham and MacInnes running off; almost immediately I got hit by some chunks of snow. I thought it was only falling ice, so I had just hunched down to protect my head when this wet snow avalanche hit me. The others say I did a bunch of slow flips before I got onto my back. The rope was wrapped around my legs, and all I could do was dog paddle on my back until I worked my way off to the side. There was gear strewn all over the place, and this big twenty-kilogram tripod I had been standing next to had its legs sheared right off. It turns out that a cornice had broken off and had set off Number Two Gully.

8
Avalanches

The Terrain

A skier can judge a slope hazardous and avoid it, but a climber may be confronted with an obvious avalanche slope and be forced to negotiate it.

Assume you are in a dead-end cirque which you must climb out of or down into. You suspect there is avalanche danger all around, but this does not mean you have to give up all control of your destiny. There are many precautions you can take to maximize your "good luck."

When confronted with any potentially dangerous slope, stop for awhile; ask yourself not only if it will slide but also what will happen if it does slide? Since you have a choice of different slopes to climb out of this cirque, you have to decide which will be the safest. Stop, think, look around, and analyze the factors that go into making one slope safe and another a death trap.

Start out by looking over the terrain. Avalanches are most common on slopes of 30 to 45 degrees. Steeper slopes tend not to collect much snow because it sloughs off. Gentler slopes need a larger load to overcome the internal cohesion of the snow. Perhaps that 55-degree gully over there on the north side is safe; maybe there is a slope that has already avalanched and is now safe. The steepest

Opposite, spindrift conditions on the north wall of the Breithorn, Switzerland. Jurgen Winkler Photo.

slopes will avalanche every few minutes during a storm and never build up a snowpack. Many a climber caught in a storm in a gully below such a slope has escaped by climbing only in between the slides that come by like clockwork. Since avalanches tend to follow couloirs and existing channels, they can act as funnels, collecting debris from cornices or masses of icicles that could break off and cause a larger slide.

The big steep ice faces and gullies in the Alps or Rockies will usually remain water-ice through the winter because of the constant sloughing off of the usual cold, dry winter snow. In the spring or during a winter thaw it is possible for snow to collect on even the steepest ice faces. That is why they are once again snow climbs in early summer. With the right conditions it is possible for even a steep wall like the north face of Mount Robson to develop a dangerous slab. The typical sequence would be: (1) the old snow or ice surface is warmed; (2) there is a warm snowfall which adheres to the old surface; (3) the temperature drops, reducing the snow density to allow a deep pack to develop; (4) a wind comes up; (5) a temperature rise weakens the slab bonding.

If you can, stay in the trees. Natural avalanches rarely *start* in dense forests or where rocks project out of the slope. It may be that the best reason for staying in the trees is that you can grab one on the way down! Keep your eyes open for scarred trees and broken tops and branches from old slides. Look around for a possible talus slope or any rough terrain to give a secure base to the snowpack. This is useful, however, only if the snowpack is relatively strong, shallow, and well bonded between layers. If the snow is very unstable, beware of the rocks and trees as false security.

The deeper the snow, the more buried the terrain irregularities—and the smoother the glide path. Prior knowledge of the terrain is invaluable. The Cairngorms in Scotland are particularly dangerous terrain for avalanches; the rounded, grassy hills offer no anchor for the snow. High pastures in the Alps are similar. The person who knows the country remembers the location of a rockslide or a cut-down forest where the snow will be well anchored.

The least avalanche danger is on ridges; there is some in valleys; but the most danger is found on the open slopes. All things being equal, a convex slope will slide before a concave one. Snow tends to be more stable in hollows, where it gets compressed; it is unstable over bumps where it is subject to tension. Avoid slopes that end in cliffs or become steeper below so that the slide can gain momentum. Look out for any crevasses or a bergschrund below where even a small slide could do you in.

This photo of a dendritic snow crystal is courtesy of the Avalanche Institute, Davos.

The Making of an Avalanche Slope

A snowslope is formed in layers of diverse snow from different storms. Each one of the layers will have different intercrystalline stability, and the bond between one layer and the next will vary in strength. After checking out the terrain and exposure you should next be concerned with the strength and stability of each one of these layers.

Eighty percent of all avalanches fall during or shortly after storms. The rate at which new snow falls is a very important factor. A heavy snowfall spread out over a few days may not be dangerous since settling will often stabilize the snow faster than it can build up. Generally, snow falling at the rate of three centimeters or more per hour is cause for concern.

The type of snow crystal falling will also have a considerable effect on the future stability of the snowpack. Snow formed at temperature extremes is often unstable; ice granules form at the warm end and needle-shaped crystals develop in extreme cold. New snow with classic *stellar* (star-shaped) or *dendritic* (branched) crystals will have considerable stability due to the interlocking of the crystal's branches and arms. Stellar crystals of a large size form at around -5 to -8 degrees C. A snow crystal which is rimed (with "furry" edges and surfaces) will have even more contact surface for interlocking and will therefore form a more initially stable snowpack. But since it won't slide until later, it can form a deeper snowpack and larger, potentially more dangerous avalanches.

If the snowfall was dendritic *without wind*, there is usually no hazard no matter what the steepness or depth of snowfall—as long as the precipitation was below approximately three centimeters per hour.

As soon as the storm clears, the steepest slopes may be bare, having slid regularly during the storm. Some of the slopes just slightly more gentle will have slid, too, maybe only once but with more volume. These soft snowslides (which can also be soft slabs), fanning out from a single trigger point, are called *point avalanches* or *loose snow avalanches*. The next gentler slopes, the ones that didn't quite slide, are the ones to watch out for. They are waiting for your extra weight to send them down.

Destructive or *equitemperature metamorphism* is the process by which the original forms of the newly fallen snow crystals gradually change to more rounded forms. Temperature will cause a transfer of the water vapor by *sublimation* from the tips of the crystal's branches to the central core. Gravity will promote compaction and settling of the snowpack. Although equitemperature metamorphism destroys the original intercrystalline bond of the stellar-type snow crystals, the compaction generally causes increased strength in the snowpack, settling and freezing the individual crystals together—this is more stable than a mere interlocking of their branches. Because the intercrystalline bond is poor in columnar and plate-like crystals, they will slough off and avalanche during and right after storms. After a day or two all but the lowest-angle slopes will have slid. Metamorphism and settling will make these slopes more stable.

Temperature is a great influence in stabilizing snowslopes. During three warm summer days a half meter of fresh snow can settle, yet three or four days of clear, windless cold might still leave twenty-five centimeters of new snow dangerously unstable.

A snow pack of light, fluffy, new snow will have great inter-crystalline strength, but after a period of persistent low temperatures this bond will be destroyed through the recrystallizing effects of steep temperature gradients in the surface snow layers. This *constructive metamorphism* or *temperature gradient metamorphism* explains why powder snow is often drier and lighter after a few days of cold weather than right after a storm. A snowfall starting with cold temperatures and dry snow and followed by warmer temperatures is likely to cause avalanches because the dry snow on the bottom is not likely to bond to the old snow, and the new, denser snow on top will result in an unstable "top-heavy" condition.

The Himalaya, with its great temperature difference between night and day and intense solar radiation, causes avalanches to occur with almost every storm. During a stormy period in the Karakoram in 1975, we noticed that the avalanches tended to be of two types: if the precipitation occurred at night, the slopes would slide at about nine or ten in the morning when the sun warmed the slopes; if precipitation occurred during the day, the avalanches would begin after the evening freeze. Timing is the key to safe movement in those mountains.

There are ways of determining the stability of a snowpack without resorting to howitzer fire. You can jump on the slope (repeatedly if necessary) to get an answer as to its stability; this jumping should be done only in a safe place! One of the best ways is to dig a pit and check out the strength of each layer and its bond to the other layers or to the ground.

Digging a pit is tiring and time-consuming but revealing and effective. A shovel makes the job easier and so does a small brush for accentuating the stratigraphys. Another invaluable tool is a ten- or twenty-power magnifying glass. This is an aid not only for looking at new snow crystals but also for checking out the shapes and strengths of the old crystals lower in the snowpack. Dig the hole as close to the potential release point as possible and dig all the way to the ground or at least to the permanent snow. Stick your finger in each layer and feel the resistance of the snow. How strong is it? Is there a super-thin layer of ice under all that new powder? Look at the snow crystals with the glass. What's their shape? Are they locked or frozen together? Perhaps there is a ball-bearing layer of *graupel* or *hail* that never consolidated from an early fall storm. What's that layer that feels like granulated sugar in your hand? It's probably *depth hoar* or *temperature gradient snow*, which forms as a result of a steep temperature difference between the relatively warm ground (or a layer such as an ice layer within the pack) and the

Below, mature depth-hoar crystals. The photo is courtesy of the Avalanche Institute, Davos.

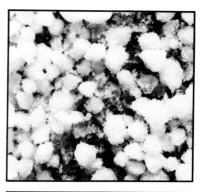

163

colder atmosphere. Depth hoar is most often formed early in the winter, when the snow cover is shallow, the ground is warm, and the air is very cold (-20 degrees Celsius or below). Though the ground may be frozen, it is never far below 0 degrees C because the snow acts as an insulator. This steep temperature gradient in such a short distance will diffuse the mass from one part of the snow cover to another. This sublimation causes the shape of the snow crystals to change and grow to where they are scroll- or cup-shaped. This shape crystal has no cohesiveness, creates air spaces in the pack, and has no strength when it gets wet or becomes crushed under the weight of another snowfall. In the United States depth hoar is commonly found in the Rocky Mountains in winter because of the cold, dry weather. It rarely occurs in the wet, warmer Cascades.

In the winter of 1967-1968, little snow fell in the Southern Andes, and the spring was warm, with many clear days. Conditions were lousy for skiing but great for climbing in the mountains around Bariloche. Some friends and I were climbing up a steep snowslope in the Cathedral Group, and, though it was very steep, we didn't feel worried about not having a rope because the steps were so sure. It was perfect *neige à bout pied* step-kicking. About halfway up something told me that not all was right with this slope. I stopped at a convenient rock and dug almost a meter down with my axe. I suddenly broke through the crust to a bottomless pit of "snow cone"-like mush, so saturated with water that I could hardly contain it in my hand. (We went rockclimbing the rest of the day!) This was a classic example of *rotten snow*, formed when a layer of depth hoar in the lower part of the snow cover becomes wet from melt or rainwater and loses what little strength it had. It frequently causes wet, loose-snow or huge slab avalanches which sweep everything down to ground level.

A *wet snow avalanche* is the most common type that the climber will face in the late spring or summer in the Alps, Alaska, or the Rockies. It is only the surface layer which is melting and avalanching and not a weak layer below the surface, as in a *wet slab avalanche*. Wet snow avalanches in the summer in the United States are usually too small to be dangerous, but even a small slide can carry you into a waiting bergschrund that is invisible from above. When wet snow stops sliding, it sets up like cement; you don't have to be buried to be immobilized. In the Alps the threat is serious enough to rule out many descent routes after the heat of the day has penetrated to a critical depth in the snowpack.

Rainstorms or spring weather with warm winds and cloudy nights can hasten the warming and melting of the snow cover. A *chinook* or *foehn* (both warm, dry winds) will melt the snow at a faster rate than any other natural heat source, including solar radiation.

Look at the base of slopes for characteristic avalanche fans. Snowballs or cartwheels rolling on their own down a slope may indicate only shallow instability. Throwing a large rock onto a slope is a questionable indicator unless it causes a slide; then you know that a person can do the same or better! A well-belayed climber can learn a good deal by his deliberate attempts to start a slide.

If the snow load is heavy, the pack is equitemperature, the air temperature is between 4 and 7 degrees C, and the slope is smooth and unmarked, you should be looking for a wet slab, especially if there are sliding surfaces present; i.e., ice layer, grass, or depth hoar.

Waiting for the afternoon or evening cold to stabilize the slope is often a good idea. Make sure you wait for real consolidation, since the freezing itself will sometimes start a slide. If the depth of the wet snow is not excessive, you can purposely start a slide and "rumpage" down with it, staying above the mass the whole way, pushing as much of the snow ahead as possible. A *runnel* (the center of a gully) on a slope may be the safest place to do this, depending on whether or not the runnel has been regularly relieving itself.

Effects of the Sun and Wind

In a cirque the various slopes will present different exposure to the sun and the wind. Snow is generally much weaker and of lower density on north rather than south-facing slopes because of the sun's radiation. In addition, an unstable slope will stabilize more quickly on the sunny slopes. If a south-facing slope is dangerous from a potential wet snow avalanche, pick a slope facing a different direction or pick a part of the snowfield or gully that receives less sun.

Wind builds *slab avalanche* conditions. It scours snow off the windward slopes, pulverizes it, and drops it off on the leeward side of the ridge. The further effect of the wind mechanically alters the grains to round spheres which are then packed close together to form a *hard slab*—the most dangerous and unpredictable of all unstable snow conditions. Hard slabs can form whenever there is high wind and low temperature. There need not be any precipitation. Hard slab is dangerous not as an unstable mass like loose snow, but because it may be adhering far better to itself than to the snow below. You can gauge the thickness and consistency of a shallow slab by probing with the ice axe. Settling of large areas is

Our best way of judging consists of knowing the influences provoking an avalanche situation and observing nature which usually shows its tricks in a generous fashion.

—*Andre Roche*
"Avalanches"
Mountain World, *1963*

This slab in the Bugaboos fractured but did not release the day after these ski tracks were made. Jim Davies Photo.

common soon after a storm; walking and stomping on a gentle slope can give an idea of how it is behaving. Instead of growing and fanning out from a single trigger point like soft, uncohesive snow does, a slab will snap off as a unit from a horizontal fracture line. A slab is held in place at the top, sides, bottom, and between the slab and the substratum. If one of these fails, the others must hold the slab in place. When you experience a settling or "whoomp," the slab probably settled and failed on a weak substratum; the other points held the slab in place. The most effective point on a slab to trigger release is in the center of the slab. This is not to say that you won't cause a release at the fracture line. It is safer for a person to cross a suspected slab in the fracture line area rather than through the middle of the slab; the person is then above the majority of the snow and is more likely to ride out on top. In any case, if you get caught in a slab avalanche, you probably set it off. Stay on the windward side of ridges to avoid *wind slab*. *Soft slab* avalanches are formed from a combination of wind and heavy snowfall, and they slide during or right after a storm. They sometimes form without regard to wind direction and may be found on windward as well as lee slopes. There is no exact distinction between hard slab and soft. Slabs come in a wide range of hardness—from those where ski tracks don't show to those which offer good powder skiing.

There is strong argument for getting to know one mountain range very well, learning its prevailing winds and typical storm cycles. Get to know local wind conditions. The prevailing wind in a particular area may come from the west during clear weather and may change to the southwest or south during a storm. Also, get to know and remember the weather and precipitation history of the present season up to the point in question. Try to develop a "continuity" feeling for the existing snowpack as related to everything that went on since it started to form. Your subconscious can this way be "programmed" to respond and give you hunches through the "seat of the pants" system. The better you know the normal conditions, the more unusual variations will stand out with their special promises and dangers.

In the long run, as the avalanche expert Ron Perla has said, "The only rule of thumb about avalanches is that there *are* no rules of thumb."

Precautions and Rescue

Even if intuition and analysis of the terrain, weather, and snow inform you which is the safest slope, there are still many things you can do to stack the deck in your favor. Before going to the mountains in the winter call the local ski area, the mountain guides, or the Forest Service and ask about the avalanche danger. Before going onto the slope each person should put on warm clothing. All equipment should be loose and free, ready to throw away. Tie in to twenty meters of brightly colored avalanche cord. Some skiers carry helium balloons on short cords. Avalanche radios are excellent for ski touring through trees, where long cords are a hindrance. The transmitter/receiver is about the size of a pack of cigarettes. Every member of the party carries one switched on to "transmit," and if someone is buried, the other sets are turned on to "receive" to locate him.

A rare summertime slab avalanche on the Loch Vale Couloir in Colorado. Water may have percolated through an old slab to a hard ice base that became lubricated. U.S. Forest Service Photo.

Don't rope up. On a narrow slope one person can be belayed from the side, but the belayer should not be tied into the rope unless he wants to try to hold a freight train. On potentially dangerous slopes only one person should move at a time. Have the escape route picked out. When going up or down, keep to the fall line; don't zigzag. In a traverse keep above the avalanche danger. Spend as little time as possible exposed to the danger—go like hell!

Although relatively few mountaineers have been caught in bad avalanches, it happens regularly enough that you should know something about getting free of them. The standard advice for those unfortunates who are caught is to "swim." Some who have done it liken it to climbing continuously toward the surface. Everyone agrees you have to fight like crazy to stay on top. Don't try to outrun it; instead, go for the sides. If buried, inhale deeply before the snow stops to make room for your chest. Try to make breathing space around your face with your arms or hands. Try to keep one arm or hand above the surface. As soon as struggling becomes futile, relax and conserve your energy and oxygen. Yoga breathing is the answer to relax your mind and body. (Houdini could stay for hours in a sealed chamber at the bottom of the East River.) Shout only when you hear the rescuers nearby.

For the victim buried in an avalanche, speedy search means survival. Although a few remarkable survivals after days of burial have been reported, the victim has only a fifty percent chance of being alive at the end of the first thirty minutes. As the snow comes to rest, it sets up into a hard mass—the victim can't dig himself out. His only link to life is his companions left on the surface. Their job begins before the avalanche has even stopped; they must watch the victim until he is out of sight, noting the last point seen and marking it. Keep watching and mark where the "last point seen" on the moving snow comes to a stop. The victim will most likely be somewhere on or near a line between these two points—probably closer to the lowest point.

When the slide stops, the next concern is for the safety of those not caught; it won't help the victim to have his searchers buried by another slide. Next, a hasty search for surface clues must be made: look for a mitten, a hat, a rucksack. Mark them. Look especially around trees or outcroppings, which might have stopped him. Shout at intervals and listen for a reply. If nothing is found, begin to probe in a seventy-by-seventy-five-centimeter grid, using willow wands, a blunted ice axe, or a ski pole with the basket pulled off. (There are some excellent ski poles that are made specifically to convert into probing poles. Every ski tourer should own these.)

This avalanche fell 2,500 meters down the south face of Dhaulagiri, traveled horizontally for 5 kilometers, went up a 200-meter ridge and then down another thousand meters to stop just short of destroying a base camp. Mike Covington Photo.

If there are only a few probers, or if the terrain is steep, the probers should stand fingertip-to-fingertip and probe first on one side of their bodies and then the other. A seventy-centimeter step is taken forward and probing continues. Stay quiet when probing and keep listening. When you find the victim, treat for shock and suffocation.

Avalanche prediction is a complex art struggling to become a science. I've only been able to touch on its main themes here and a little knowledge of such unpredictable forces can certainly be dangerous. I strongly recommend every aspiring alpinist to read and study all he can on the subject.

Avalanches

In 1968 five of us "fun-hogs" drove an old van from California down to the tip of South America. Our plan was to climb the fabled Fitzroy, a huge fang which rises close by the Patagonian icecap. For two months we surfed the long Pacific waves that break along the west coast of Mexico, Central America, and Peru. In Lima we sold our surfboards and headed to Chile to ski. They were having

Doug Tompkins Photo.

a drought, and Portillo had no snow; we continued south and climbed and skied down two volcanos, Mount Orsorno and Mount Llayma. Finally, after four months of travel, we crossed the Andes and arrived at the end of the road. Our gear was loaded onto some army horses, and we headed for basecamp.

Fitzroy had been climbed only twice before—the first time by the great French climbers Lionel Terray and Guido Magnone. It was one of two climbs that Terray had said he would never do again (the north face of the Eiger being the other). Our plan was to race to the peak, do a new route alpine style—getting all five of us to the top—and film the entire adventure. A pretty bold and audacious plan but, after all, Fitzroy is only 3,700 meters high.

Well, we ran into a problem with the weather. Of the sixty days we were there we had only five days of good weather. Consequently, we were forced to yo-yo up and down the mountain; this put a lot of wear and tear on our equipment, which was designed only for normal alpine climbing.

It was early in the season and the snows were deep and wet. Our gaiters didn't protect our boots very well, and so the boots were the first piece of equipment to break down. It wasn't long before the leather wouldn't stay waterproof—the stitching quickly rotted. The soles of Chris Jones' new boots began to delaminate!

Most of the time the wind was so strong that we had to live in ice caves to get away from the awful noise. Besides, no tent could have held up. Living in caves for thirty-one days presented some special problems with our down gear. As soon as we lit the stove, the humidity would rise to near-saturation level, and our sleeping bags and down jackets soaked up the dampness. Naturally, there was no way to dry either these items or our boots, which by now were getting moldy.

Several of our fixed ropes were ruined when we didn't leave enough slack between the anchors. After one seventeen-day storm we returned to find the ropes shrunk. One forty-six-meter rope was now about forty-two meters long, and it was so tight that we had to cut it loose because the knots were like iron.

When the summit day finally came, our anoraks and woolen breeches were in tatters, our wretched boots were frozen solid, and our bivouac gear was left in the cave soaking wet. We climbed for twenty-three straight hours to the summit and back; it was a race with both the weather and our deteriorating equipment. Had we been caught by a storm high on the mountain, we would have been in bad trouble. Not having the bivouac gear forced us to move quickly and continuously.

Back at basecamp we all agreed that the equipment had let us down, and we swore right there to pay more attention in the future. Fortunately, in the next few years there were some radical changes in gaiters and clothing, to mention only a few items.

9
Equipment

Tools and Technology

Going to the mountains in the first place is an admission that personal effort is taking precedence over mechanical means. A mountaineer chooses to make this effort in a simple and fairly unstructured environment. Similarly, the modern climber is letting simplicity guide him in his selection of mountain gear.

I would not wish to imply that the gear used in climbing ice is not high technology. Just looking at the climbing rope with its continuous nylon filaments carefully woven for tremendous shock absorption would quickly dispel any such notion. But I think climbers are now consciously reducing the number and complexity of climbing aids. Even the rope is used only as a safety backup while the climber tries to ascend without its assistance. Though climbers seek simplicity in the mountains, tool-making and envy of new gadgets are a part of our way of life. Climbers will sometimes lose sight of their simple goal while tinkering with a raft of gadgets for easy ascent. There is no end in sight to the number of more highly developed climbing aids for ever more specialized uses.

One of the real attractions of ice climbing is that the same few tools which are needed for easy climbs will also take the mountaineer through some of the hardest passages, once he applies technique, judgment, and boldness. Once he is outfitted to withstand the climate of the mountains, very little else will be needed to take him climbing. Rope, ice axe, and crampons—these are the heart of the snow and ice mountaineer's kit.

These few, simple tools share with the climber's clothes a need for versatility. If they were not so adaptable, the tools would never cover such a wide range of climbing techniques in mountain situations ranging over the face of the earth. The same ice axe should serve for wallowing in Himalayan snows, probing for crevasses in Alaska, clawing water-ice in Montana, anchoring a belay in French névé, or cutting through an Andean cornice. One tool —many jobs. Versatility is the byword, and simplicity the key. Each special function is blended into the overall design.

The climber must depend absolutely on the few tools he does choose. The sudden loss of an ice axe could be fatal. Of course, this means not dropping it, but it also must not break; the tool must be well made. The more the things around us are built to a temporary standard, and the more we see and deal with it in our cars, houses, and clothes (and come to expect things to break and fall apart as fast as they go out of fashion), the harder it will be for us to recognize quality, know and demand it, and be willing to pay its price. A person can go down to the 98¢ bin at the corner hardware and buy a hammer that will pound nails—for a while. But it will surely break suddenly in the middle of a job, leaving an unfinished work and another piece of junk to add to the world's collection. Of course, it would be more than an inconvenience to break that hammer on the Ice Hose Pitch of the Eiger. How much better it would be to have a good tool at ten times the price, a tool you would get to know as the years went on until it settled naturally into your grip. You may even have the pleasure of passing a good tool on to someone eager to learn its use, and the art along with it.

A very practical consequence of simplified alpinism is mobility. A light load makes an agile climber. Unencumbered, you can climb faster, your range is extended to longer climbs, and more time is free for work on difficult passages.

Boots

The ice axe may be mountaineering's symbol, but good boots are its foundation. A well-shod climber will be able to go a long way on footwork before he has to bring his axe into play. Many good ice axes are available and have only to be paid for, but a good pair of boots is getting harder to find at any price. They should always be made from the best unsplit hides of mature cattle, but time is money and it is more economical to split a hide into several thinner layers and build a boot that is both floppier and inherently less waterproof. As soon as a boot begins to be recognized for the quality of its leather and construction, the demand goes up; soon that very quality begins to suffer. Finding a good boot is something of a black art, and if ever you do find a good pair that fit your feet, buy two pairs, because the quality will never be the same again.

A boot for climbing snow and ice should have similar characteristics to a boot used for steep rockclimbing; the most important requirement is a stiff sole that offers protection for the feet. In slab or friction climbing a certain amount of flexibility in the sole is desirable. The soles are either laid flat on the granite for more adhesion or they "edge" over the bones of the balls of the feet on tiny flakes; the feet are splayed sideways in perfect Charlie Chaplin style. On limestone or dolomite walls the climbing is characteristically vertical, and the sharp-edged holds are generally horizontal. If you try to edge on the side of the boot, your body will be too close to the rock and therefore out of balance. You need to get away from the steepness and stand on the tips of your toes. Similarly, if you want to climb steep ice, then you had better have boots with stiff soles.

I have had some outstanding boots that took months—even several climbers—to break in. In fact, this process might more realistically be thought of as breaking the feet into the boots. These boots were made of leather—thick, good-quality leather—and each pair lasted me for several hard seasons.

Once molded to the foot, a good boot becomes all things to the alpinist: it's stiff enough for front-pointing, yet it bends just a little under the toes for granite friction; it's close-cropped at the welt for delicate edging on erratic boulders in an alpine meadow. For the long walk back down to the roadhead the toes are kept from blistering by a firm fit through the instep and heel. A slight curve, known as a rocker, is built into the boot sole like the cut of a wooden shoe to take the sting out of stiff-soled trail kilometers. In the winter good boots can fit into alpine touring bindings for ski mountaineering; with Arlberg straps to stiffen up the ankles, the boots work quite well through the powder in the trees.

Beware of boots that are loaded with foam padding, have fashionable scree collars running all the way down to the heel, or have soft, thin (or split) leather uppers. These are tourist boots made to

To cut a step in ice is obviously uncomplicated, and you can fashion it to suit your own taste—soup plates for big feet and mantle-shelfing, or 'God save all here' jughandles. It is an art form, and self expression is rare indeed in mountaineering. It only becomes a mountaineering skill when you have the ability to cut a few gross or to do without when there isn't enough ice. However, this approach is only applicable to the historic romantic period which prevailed before the sixties, for the last decade has 'done for' the bold committed leads of bygone days, when the knickerbocker brigade would lead up a hundred feet of ice secured only by a dessicated old ice-axe belay. Now, with technological ravages typical of the modern mind, you can hardly get near the ice for the mass of gear to be carried—staves, screws, deadmen, curving pick hammers, axes, whistles, pieces, clinometers, etc. Second men would be better trained as caddies, or building Yosemite prams to trail up the ice walls. This is possibly 'sour grapes,' for I also carry some of these items, but confess to finding them singularly useless!

—Jimmy Marshall
Mountain

Equipment

break in over one weekend—and break down before the end of the expedition.

Fifteen to eighteen centimeters is a good height for a boot; more binds the ankles which must stay flexible for good French technique. But even at that height, the uppers can be too stiff and will unnecessarily restrain the free bending of the ankle. This is a delicate point. The over-the-ankle height is necessary to keep the heel firmly into the back of the boot and generally keep the ankle from turning under on long, tiring descents. But it must also bend fore and aft for the motion of walking. Some side-to-side flexibility is absolutely essential for *pied à plat* technique, slab climbing, and minimizing awkwardness on talus slopes caused by the stiff soles. This compromise between flexibility and support can be achieved by the use of good leather, stiffeners, and proper design. Stay away from gimmicks like hinged heels and stiff ankle cups. Double boots offer no ankle flexibility at all, since they stiffen through friction of the inner against the outer boot. This makes them good for ski mountaineering, but for climbing they are cumbersome and not much warmer than a loose-fitting pair of good single boots with two pairs of socks and a pair of Supergators. A major cause of cold feet is a lack of circulation caused by wearing too small a boot or too many socks. Boots with bellows tongues and soft uppers will cut off circulation in the large blood vessels that lie close to the surface on top of the arch. (Crampon straps will do the same.) A far warmer boot is one with an overlapping tongue closure made out of good, stiff leather so the foot is free to move around. The lacing system should be as snagproof as possible; a climber poised between the earth and the sky cannot afford to be tripping over his shoelaces. Especially bad is a currently fashionable lacing hook low down on the side of the ankle.

If a boot is truly waterproof, it does not breathe, and therefore the perspiration from your feet will be absorbed by the socks and by the inside leather and foam padding of the boot. As long as you can dry your socks and boots every night, this is no problem. But this is often impossible on long climbs and expeditions. For these situations I will wear a medium-thick sock next to my skin, then put on a thin plastic bag and a thick wool sock over that. I find that this method has a double advantage in that it keeps my boots and thick socks bone dry and my feet stay a bit warmer.

Clothing

For *breeches*, *sweaters*, *shirts*, and *caps*, the answer is wool. For wet conditions typical of snow climbing, wool is still the best material.

Even though it absorbs water, it retains its dead-air structure when wet. The wily Scots wear wool to obtain body friction in icy chimneys and cracks. One clever climber who suddenly found himself in a crevasse without benefit of crampons extracted himself by taking off his boots and freezing his wool socks to the vertical ice as he patiently bridged out.

Sweaters, long johns, and mittens made of noncellular synthetic fabrics such as polyesters and acrylics are beginning to appear; they absorb little water and dry quickly with just body heat. A garment made of this material has the advantage of being much lighter than wool and, of course, it's warmer in wet conditions. In the near future we will see more of these new fabrics for mountain clothing.

A day spent in the wet arctic winter winds of Scotland will turn any wool-dressed climber into a solid popsicle. When you don't need the friction properties of wool, use a wind or rain anorak and pants to prevent this "picturesque" situation. Remember, though, if the snow won't stick to your nylon clothing, you won't stick to the snow. There have been some terribly nasty falls from glissading in windsuits. In fact, many ski areas will not allow skiers to wear slick "wet-look" clothing on the slopes.

Clothes should be loose-fitting enough to allow the freedom and precision of movement that ice climbing demands. Gaiters and wind pants should be somewhat snug and streamlined so they don't snag the points of passing crampons. Keeping the head warm with a wool cap, scarf, or balaclava is surprisingly important. Your head is only twenty percent of your body's surface area, yet, having no protective layer of fat like the rest of the body, it can radiate away forty percent of your heat. Several layers of insulation will keep you warmer than a single layer and make you more adaptable to variations in temperature and exertion. Wool doesn't generate any heat, it only preserves what is already there. And while it is true that cold feet dictate another sweater, ultimately you must produce more heat to stay warm. This means food, and the colder the weather, the more you must eat. I have become nauseated from starting on a winter climb without enough breakfast. Extra fats and carbohydrates are especially needed for the body to adapt to cold weather: butter in the oatmeal, salami, cheese, and nuts. A pocketful of munchies staves off the numbing inactivity at belay stances.

Gloves or *mittens* must not only keep your hands warm and dry but also provide a good grip on your ice axe. For normal summer use I prefer either soft, unlined leather gloves or, better yet, gloves

Think of everything you could possibly want on a climbing expedition, say, of thirty hours. Cut out from this all that you think might be fairly easily dispensed with. Take with you 50 per cent of the remainder.

—Harold Raeburn
Mountaineering Art

Equipment

made of rubber-covered fabric. These keep your hands adequately warm for even light winter use and are less constricting than padded ski gloves. They also give an unexcelled grip and allow good finger dexterity for rockclimbing or gripping a slippery ice axe shaft. For colder conditions wear light wool gloves underneath and carry spare pairs to replace them as they get wet. For extreme conditions wool gloves inside heavy, oiled wool mittens inside waterproof overmitts provide the most warmth—but you'll have a clumsier grip on the ice axe. For mixed climbing I often wear fingerless gloves inside Dachstein mitts. The mittens can be tied to the sleeve of the sweater with a cord or large safety pin to allow their removal while using only gloves.

A *gaiter* should extend down from the knee and cover as much of the boot as possible. The material should be waterproof over the boot but breathable around the leg to avoid condensation on the inside. The best gaiters are those invented by Peter Carman and called Supergators. They cinch around the welt and are waterproof and insulated. They perform the same function as overboots but leave the soles exposed for rockclimbing. Supergators are nearly as warm as double boots and are lighter and less awkward. They will keep your boots dry even in the peat bogs of Scotland.

Other Items and Advice

Leather or nylon *crampon straps* will stretch and freeze when wet. Hemp will shrink when wet, cutting circulation and causing cold feet; neoprene-covered nylon makes the best strap. Stay away from the new, quick, mechanical lacing systems. None of them are foolproof; I've seen the best of these come flying off a boot in the middle of a hard ice pitch. In the fastest, simplest, and most foolproof lacing system, one strap threads completely around the ankle for extra support; the other strap goes through the front rings from the *outside* of the ring to the *inside*. Not only does this system self-lock for a more secure fastening that could delay disaster from a broken strap, but it does not have to be laced as tightly over the toes, which will thus stay warmer. Make sure the buckles are on the outside of the foot and cut off the loose strap ends that might trip you. Remember that climbers don't get chopped from great heroic falls while trying impossibly hard overhanging pitches—they get killed for reasons like tripping over themselves on a 40-degree snowslope. Make sure your crampons fit well, that the straps are strong (inspect them before every climb), and that the lacing system is secure. Don't leave any half hitches or long ends dangling, and watch out for baggy gaiters or pants in which you could crampon yourself.

Above, a good example of an accident waiting to happen. The front points are too short, and the strap system is a disaster. Below, proper lacing of crampon straps.

Whatever strap system you use, make sure it's fast and efficient. I've been with some very experienced climbers who have taken fifteen or twenty minutes to take their crampons out of their pack, pull off the point protectors, put them on their boots, and make adjustments on the straps that should have been done at home. In that time they could have cut steps across the ice patch and been far ahead of the game.

On winter climbs or summer expeditions to the high mountains a good *shovel* will be invaluable. It can be used for digging snow pits, ice caves, or snowshelters, or for digging out an avalanche victim. With a shovel, security is always at hand. Not only is a shovel lighter than a tent but it's more versatile. In an area like the southern Andes of Patagonia you often can't use a tent because of the high winds. When we climbed Fitzroy in 1968, we were pinned down in an ice cave by a terrible storm for thirteen straight days. A tent could not have withstood that storm for even one day. Some of the famous disasters of Himalayan climbing in which entire parties perished in great storms could have been averted had they been carrying shovels.

The shovel I have is a little beauty I picked up in a hardware store in Argentina. It has a steel pan and a short wooden handle. It's far stronger than cheap aluminum models and will dig holes even in ice. John Evans wrote, after he climbed the incredibly long and difficult Hummingbird Ridge of Canada's Mount Logan: "The shovel technique, which had been worked out to a science, was the key to our progress. The leader, rarely taking his ice axe out of his pack, used ice hammer, pickets, rock pitons, and the scoop shovel. With the latter he could quickly knock off the smaller cornices or with a single stroke produce a splendid bucket step in the crisp snow."

While wallowing in the spring thaw sometime, you might give thought to the potential of *skis* on all kinds of soft snow. Skiing is the solution to several maddening problems—from just plain deep softness, to breakable crust and rotten snow which only reveals its full horrors to the climber on foot. Salewa of Munich makes skis especially for high-mountain touring. They are wider and shorter (120 centimeters) than alpine or crosscountry skis. Used with bindings that convert from walking to downhill position, and skins or waxes, they are ideal for soft spring snow. I would never climb Mont Blanc or Mount Rainier early in the season without a pair of these to take me down.

One of the most necessary tools of the alpine climber is his *headlamp*. Without it, alpine starts are impossible except on moonlit nights.

Keep the batteries close to the body where they can be warm; they are four times more efficient at body temperature than at freezing.

If you use a grinder to *sharpen your tools*, don't allow the steel to overheat and turn color; this will soften the temper and ruin the points. For long climbs or expeditions you should carry a file, and the one I prefer is a double-ended, three-corner mill file. File the front points of crampons only from the top at a straight angle; the adze of an ice axe is filed only on the bottom, also at a straight angle. Crampon side points are filed only on the front and back sides, keeping a straight angle. I file my tools razor sharp, then dull them a bit to keep the edge from bending over.

Opposite, Niki and Ian Clough traversing the lower ice slope on the north face of the Matterhorn. John Cleare Photo.

Equipment

In the 1950s the goal of every Alpine climber was to do one or more of the great north walls in the Alps—the Matterhorn, Eiger, or Grandes Jorasses. In the States there was but one north wall and that was on the Grand Teton. It had seen very few ascents, and most of these had involved a bivouac somewhere on the mountain. Those fortunate few who managed an ascent came back with stories of terrible rockfall, iced-over rocks, routefinding problems, and all the usual troubles one finds on a typical big north wall. It was the premier American alpine climb, and, of course, was a dream of mine ever since I began climbing in 1955.

Around 1957 Barry Corbet and I were hired to carry loads for a photographer who was doing a story on the climb for *Life*. Two heavily laden horses were unloaded at Amphitheater Lake, and the gear was transferred onto our two backs. For twenty-five dollars each we were to carry camping gear for the summit team along the Black Dike and all the way to the Upper Saddle, a distance of several kilometers and an elevation gain of a thousand meters. Barry carried his share in one monster load, but I made two trips with mine. The ordeal remains the most exhausting day I've ever spent in the mountains. But we made it to the saddle by nightfall and even went so far as to set up the tents and lay out the sleeping bags for the summit climbers. We knew they would arrive exhausted. Well, one of the climbers, Hans Kraus, was so impressed by our efforts that he later sent us each a brand new kernmantle rope, perhaps the first ones to appear in the States.

A couple of days later I was invited to traverse out onto the north face to help reshoot the Pendulum Pitch. We traversed the Owen-Spaulding Route until it turned into the Second Ledge of the North Face Route. The Teton guide Dick Pownall even allowed me to lead the key pitch of the traverse, a rotten, ice-covered gully. I couldn't believe my luck to be climbing with such famous climbers on the north face and even be asked to lead!

Later on, in August, 1958, I finally got the courage to attempt the whole climb. Jack Davis and I got a pre-dawn start to avoid the rockfall which comes off the right side of the face, hits the Grandstand, and splatters all over the base of the route. We roped up for the bergschrund but, since the climbing seemed easy above, took it off until we reached the slimy Guano Chimney just below the First Ledge. Here we found and used several of Paul Petzoldt's old strap-iron pitons, placed by him on the first ascent. The face was dry and we easily skirted the icefield on the ledge. We didn't have many problems getting over the Pendulum Pitch or the infamous Traverse into the V. Before we knew it, we were standing on the summit; it had taken less than six hours.

A few days later I was in a bookstore in Jackson when I overheard some people talking about the recent fast ascent of the north face. It felt very satisfying to have realized a dream and to have succeeded in every way. But our achievement was flawed—it had been too easy. The Ideal that had been in my mind proved to be too far from Reality. It's like lusting over the perfect, untouchable woman: sometimes it's better not to catch up with her. Right then I decided to make the north face of the Grand the perfect climb.

I waited until after a big storm in late September, 1959 to return to the wall, this time with Ken Weeks and Fred Beckey. The face was plastered from top to bottom with snow and ice. We climbed unroped over the lower sections, but it wasn't long before we had to put on crampons. The Petzoldt pitons now shone at me through a sheet of dirty black ice. It was cold—well below freezing— and at times I had to kick my feet around to restore circulation. We weren't able to do the Direct Finish because of a huge mass of ice which blocked the start of the Traverse into the V. It was almost dark when we reached the summit, and the sky was jet black when we crawled into a cave to escape the terrible wind. I've been on a hundred bivouacs since, but this was the coldest night I've ever spent. We had no proper bivouac gear and so stayed awake all night to massage our feet. When at last dawn came, we unlimbered our stiff and tired bodies and descended to the valley.

A couple of years later Janie Taylor did the face in shorts and klettershoes, but that's all right. I've also gotten what I wanted from the north face.

Tom Frost Photo

10
Style and Ethics

The Challenge

We are *Homo sapiens*, the tool users. We earn the name by developing tools to increase our leverage on the world around us, and with this increased technological leverage comes a growing sense of power. This position of advantage which protects us from wild nature we call civilization. Our security increases as we apply more leverage, but along with it we notice a growing isolation from the earth. We crowd into cities which shut out the rhythms of the planet—daybreak, high tide, wispy cirrus high overhead yelling storm tomorrow, moonrise, Orion going south for the winter. Perceptions dull and we come to accept a blunting of feeling in the shadow of security. Drunk with power, I find that I am out of my senses. I, tool man, long for immediacy of contact to brighten my senses again, to bring me nearer the world once more; in my security I have forgotten how to dance.

So, in reaction, we set sail on the wide sea without motors in hopes of feeling the wind; we leave the Land Rover behind as we seek the desert to know the sun, searching for a remembered bright world. Paddling out again, we turn to ride the shorebreak landward, walking on the waves, the smell of wildflowers meeting us on the offshore breeze. In the process we find not what our tools can do for us but what we are capable of feeling without them, of

Opposite, Paul Braithwaite and Jeff Lowe soloing on Ben Nevis. Piolet traction is being used where it belongs here.

knowing directly. We learn how far our unaided effort can take us into the improbable world. Choosing to play this game in the vertical dimensions of what is left of wild nature makes us climbers. Only from the extreme of comfort and leisure do we return willingly to adversity. Climbing is a symptom of post-industrial man.

Some climbers claim that using modern equipment and techniques (like *piolet traction*) diminishes the adventure to be found on the classic ice climbs. What these climbers forget, however, is that the curved ice axe, rigid crampons, and *piolet traction* were specifically designed for climbing steeper and harder ice in better style. They were *not* designed to "overkill" the standard difficulties of the classic routes. Tools can, and have, eliminated the need for sophisticated techniques and varied experience. Instead of practicing techniques and slowly working their way up to the classic routes, climbers nowadays are in a hurry, and the latest-model tools can indeed make these routes easier. Most physically fit people can learn to haul themselves up vertical ice on their first day with crampons, and, as a consequence, ice climbing is becoming popular. Inevitably, this means that the specialized tools will be abused and that the true adventure of ice climbing can be lost.

On ice the manner in which you climb is not so important to others as it is on rock, where climbing in poor style can ruin the route for future parties, sometimes permanently (as in the case of unnecessary bolting). Ice is a renewable resource, and no one should care what you do with it. Even a line of bucket steps will be melted smooth in a day or two. But still, the respect of our peers is important, and if for nothing else than our own satisfaction and enjoyment, we must set up rules for the game so at least we don't delude ourselves.

Changing the Rules

A climber disappointed with the trivial difficulties of the classic climbs and bored with the repetitiousness of front-pointing has some alternatives. He can do the climbs in more difficult conditions, in better style, or he can do harder climbs.

More difficult conditions can be found in winter or in midsummer of a bad-weather year. A few years ago the big snow and ice faces in the Alps were considered "out of condition" when they turned to ice in August. Now some climbers don't consider them "in condition" until they *do* turn icy.

Winter conditions mean dealing with difficult approaches, heavier packs, avalanche danger, brittle ice, and numbing cold. Since con-

ditions on ice climbs vary so greatly from summer to winter or even from one day to the next, it seems senseless to attempt to rate them. If you ran up Scotland's Zero Gully when it was in perfect snow/ice conditions and thought it was overrated, go back sometime when it's covered with thin, clear ice and you can't get any protection on the first pitch.

Doing a climb in better style can mean not cutting steps, eliminating artificial aid, using less equipment, or climbing alone.

Solo climbing need not be a dance with death or even a "desperate" way to climb anymore. In fact, it may prove to be the safest and most logical way for the expert ice climber to do the classic climbs. Being strapped into well-placed tools in *piolet traction* provides enough of a self-belay to more than justify not using a rope belay on a standard climb that is in reasonable condition. The rope offers mainly psychological protection anyway on early season snow climbs and gives no protection from avalanches or falling rocks and icicles. Besides, I would rather be unroped than have to climb together with a climber of dubious ability.

Henry Barber and Rob Taylor on the beginning of the 150-meter-long Vettefossen, Norway. Tomas Carlstrom Photo.

The greatest of the Scottish solo ice climbers, Tom Patey, has written a most literate (though hardly serious) plea for solo climbing in his book, *One Man's Mountains*:

> Once in a while it is very refreshing to climb alone. The practice is traditionally indefensible. I will therefore attempt to defend it. There are two cardinal precepts in mountaineering: (1) the leader must not fall, (2) the leader must climb as if the rope was not there. The first commandment is self-evident. No useful purpose could be served by a leader falling except to provide his followers with belaying practice. For the second commandment, there is only one way to ensure that a leader climbs as if his rope was not there—take away the rope. Now, it is also a fact that two men climbing unroped are no more secure than one. Ergo—the best solution is to climb solo.

The most difficult ice route has not yet been climbed. It may be a black-ice gully in the Himalaya, a frozen thousand-meter-high waterfall in Alaska, or a vertical wall of rime in the Arctic. In any case, there are always more difficult climbs you can do. The frustrated Scottish climber can find all the new gullies and ice smears he wants in Norway. The hidden couloirs and ice runnels of the Alpine winter have hardly been touched. In other words, there are still plenty of opportunities for the creative climber who wants to beat his own drum.

For those who prefer to stick to the established climbs, the rules of the game must be constantly updated to keep up with the expanding technology. Otherwise we overkill the classic climbs and delude ourselves into thinking we are better climbers than the pioneers.

The technological imperative of industrial man has always been that if it *can* be done it *should* be done. There is no choosing; if it's possible it must be right. Modern man, enslaved by his technical imagination, is shoveling coal to a runaway locomotive. But technology should set him free, opening choices instead of dictating them. Declining a possible technology is the first step toward freedom from this bondage—and returning human values to control. The whole direction of climbing moves against the technological gradient. Here personal qualities like initiative, boldness, and technique are supported rather than suppressed by the tools of the trade.

In the last few years, as I became more sure of myself and more poised in balance on the ice, I found myself stretching technique. For instance, I used only the ice axe for clawing in steeper and more brittle situations. My Alpine hammer stayed holstered for whole pitches and climbs. This is the technological inversion: fewer tools applied with increasing delicacy. I was rewarded for walking this edge by seeing more sharply what was around me, and I felt more deeply what comes boiling up from within. Thoreau put it that "simplification of means and elevation of ends is the goal." They can't help happening together. The rockclimber moves in this same direction as he works his way from artificial to free climbing, from using pitons to the less secure but more natural protection of clean climbing. Many of the classic routes are being depitoned, and climbers are forced to find their own way and place their own natural protection.

What is happening now in ice climbing is a temporary imbalance in values. The ice revolution has brought all this new technology, but climbers really haven't yet learned to control it. Some think it would be a regression in the art to do the classics with only an ice axe and crampons. But actually the loss of security afforded by that extra axe or hammer would have to be replaced by genuine technique, and you would have to relearn that sense of balance and adhesion that is the key to natural ice climbing.

It would be nice if man could climb on ice as freely as the ape climbs trees and rock. Unfortunately, ice is not a natural medium for man. To perform on it, he needs his tools and equipment. When ice climbers finally do sort out their technology, they will regain that physical freedom so characteristic of free climbing on rock—that sense of every move leading to a fresh problem, a new geometry always to be worked out. Along with this freedom, the ice climber will earn a modern dividend—the rare privilege of being far from the madding crowd.

Index